5.00

5.00

THE BATTLE OF BRITAIN
PORTRAITS
OF THE FEW

Published in 2011 by Fighting High Ltd, 23 Hitchin Road, Stotfold, Hitchin, Herts, SG5 4HP.
www.fightinghigh.com

Copyright © Fighting High Ltd, 2011
Copyright text © Christopher Yeoman 2011
Foreword text © Geoffrey Wellum 2011
Illustrations by David Pritchard
Copyright illustrations © Bob Yeoman 2011

British Library Cataloguing-in-Publication data. A CIP record for this title is available from the
British Library.
ISBN −13: 978-0956269645

Designed by Michael Lindley
www.truthstudio.co.uk

Photograph of Pilot Officer H.C Adams' grave
(Page 120-121) by Sarah Medway

Printed and bound by Toppan Printing Co. (UK) Ltd.

THE BATTLE OF BRITAIN
PORTRAITS
OF THE FEW

CHRISTOPHER YEOMAN & DAVID PRITCHARD
FOREWORD BY SQUADRON LEADER
GEOFFREY WELLUM, DFC

FH

Contents

To Leonard Adlam & Delphine Hayes
Alis nocturnis

Foreword

SO MANY BOOKS HAVE BEEN WRITTEN AND PUBLISHED CONCERNING THE Battle of Britain, some better than others and many controversial. It is, therefore, most refreshing to come across a new approach to the subject in *Fighting High's The Battle of Britain: Portraits of the Few*. Many of the portraits depicted here are of fighter pilots who were known to me personally, so I can honestly vouch for the accuracy of their portrayal. They represent typical young men of my generation, and turning these pages seems to roll back the years to those days when, in 1940, I served and flew with them on the same interceptions. Their faces look back at me again, composed and totally reconciled to the prospect of yet another day of aerial combat and a job to be done; the defence of their homeland against an utterly ruthless enemy regime, bent on invasion. Christopher Yeoman and David Pritchard present a most entertaining book that will grace any collection and is an absolute 'must' for future and present generations.

Squadron Leader Geoffrey Wellum, DFC

Preface

TEN MINUTES BEFORE MY FAMILY WERE DUE TO LEAVE THE HOUSE, THE telephone rang. A big grin crossed my Dad's face as he was greeted by the voice of Flight Lieutenant John Greenwood, calling from his home in Australia. He had phoned to wish us good luck, hoping that the day's signing event at the Farnborough Air Sciences Trust Museum in Hampshire would be a great success. It was 14 October 2007, and the warm gesture was greatly appreciated as my family set off for the museum in a hurry.

On arrival I noticed a line of people queuing outside the Trenchard House two hours before the event was even due to begin. The white, historical building was a fitting location to hold a signing session, and something rather special was in the cool morning air. The excited enthusiasts talked among themselves, holding plastic folders containing aviation prints and bags of books in their hands, patiently waiting to meet the guests of honour. While final preparations were being made, the queue grew longer, and soon enough voices turned to whispers as Wing Commander John Freeborn was ushered into the museum. Several people, their faces bright with smiles, greeted John as he passed by.

Not long after, the museum was privileged to welcome seven more Battle of Britain heroes – namely, Wing Commander Tom Neil, Group Captain Billy Drake, Air Commodore Pete Brothers, Wing Commander Bob Doe, Flight Lieutenant Mike Croskell, Group Captain Byron Duckenfield and Flight Lieutenant Richard Jones.

Just after eleven o'clock, the distinguished pilots were starting to make their way towards a large wooden table in the Trenchard Room, where the Royal Air Force had originally been formed. As I entered the room, I saw Pete Brothers and Byron Duckenfield sitting next to each other, catching up on lost time. They had served together in No. 32 Squadron all those years ago, but they had not seen each other in over fifty years.

As I wandered around the corridor, Tom Neil's cheerful countenance caught my attention, and, after shaking hands, we spoke about the rugby, particularly pleased that England had beaten France in the World Cup the night before. Once all of these wonderful men were positioned at the table, surrounded by David Pritchard's watercolour paintings of themselves as handsome young fighter pilots, I took a photograph, wanting to capture this moment for ever. Being in the same room as men of the Battle of Britain is truly an honour, a privilege and always a humbling experience.

Christopher Yeoman

Introduction

As the 70th anniversary of the Battle of Britain was honoured, much was written about the great men who served during that legendary period of aerial conflict. As a personal tribute to those who gallantly flew and fought for the freedom of Britain in 1940, I have written a short story to accompany each fighter pilot whom David Pritchard, an artist and close family friend, has portrayed. The portraits were commissioned by my father several years ago, and they have since developed into prints, which are being collected all over the world by many aviation and Second World War enthusiasts. The original paintings are with each respective pilot portrayed in this book. I have also used selected combat reports, because these reports were generally penned or typed out immediately after a pilot had returned from an operational sortie. A fighter pilot's combat report really illustrates a raw and authentic picture of the action, so I have used these reports where possible. Please note that sometimes, to remain true to source, unavoidable inconsistency has therefore resulted when referring to the same Messerschmitt aircraft; basically with regard the use of 'Me' and 'Bf'.

It is well publicised that the Battle of Britain is said to have officially begun on 10 July 1940 and to have ended on 31 October 1940, but there was aerial conflict between the RAF and the Luftwaffe before and indeed after this period of time that affected the majority of the pilots involved in this book. Although I have attempted to categorise each pilot into a respective timeframe and into the order of the Battle's phases, some experiences fall slightly outside the official Battle of Britain dates.

During 1940, the Air Ministry commissioned war artist Cuthbert Orde to sketch some of the RAF's fighter pilots. After travelling around various stations and having met many of 'The Few' during the Battle of Britain, Orde remarked: 'The most striking thing about the fighter pilots is their ordinariness. Just you, I, us and Co. – ordinary sons of ordinary parents from ordinary homes.' Indeed, to look at Orde's work is to look back in time and see such ordinary young men of whom he spoke. The same feeling is invoked when looking at David

Pritchard's portraits of 'The Few' today. They were just young men from different backgrounds, many of them fresh-faced and inexperienced, but their labours will for ever be remembered for changing the course of history.

Today, when we think of an RAF fighter pilot who flew in the Second World War, we might picture a dashing young man dressed in a smart blue uniform, full of confidence, wit and charm. We might imagine a gentleman, full of courage, discipline and determination. Although this is a broad generalisation, you have only to look at squadron photographs or speak to any of the surviving veterans today to see that this would be an accurate description. But, though they might have been similar in appearance, in actual fact 'The Few' were young men from all walks of life but with one common ambition – to fly. When the Battle of Britain was in progress, Fighter Command's squadrons consisted of different types of individuals. Some had been educated in private schools; others in state schools. Some had trained with the Auxiliary Air Force; others with the RAF Volunteer Reserve. The RAF's need for pilots was great, so as a consequence experience levels among the men was very varied. Some had been very experienced pilots before the war; others had barely left Flying Training School before being posted to an active fighter squadron; but all would do their part.

On 20 August 1940, Winston Churchill delivered a stirring speech to the House of Commons in respect of the fighter pilots who were currently engaged in the cause of protecting Britain from a Nazi invasion. Churchill boldly declared that 'never was so much owed by so many to so few'. It is from this very speech that those who fought during the Battle of Britain have now become known as 'the few'.

While gathering information for this book I have been fortunate enough to have listened to first-hand accounts of some of the Battle of Britain pilots' memories and to have received letters in relation to their experiences. One of these letters in response to my own modestly stated:

You laid great stress on what a hero I was and am. Not so. I, like others, was simply at the right place at the right time and at approximately the right age. The real heroes were the many who were killed, maimed or burnt almost to death, carrying with them the scars of battle to their life's end.

While this statement is poignantly accurate, I am still guilty of calling all of those awe-inspiring men who fought against an imposing enemy, our heroes.

The Battle of Britain

IN THE SPRING OF 1940, GERMAN FORCES had spread throughout most of Western Europe with lightning speed and unmatched efficiency. In March 1939 Germany invaded and annexed Czechoslovakia, before attacking Poland on 1 September that same year. In response to this attack, the British and French governments declared war on Germany. On 3 September 1939, the British Prime Minister, Neville Chamberlain, announced to the British public that they had exhausted all attempts of peace talks with Hitler and that they were

now at war with Germany. Undoubtedly the declaration of war caused quite a stir among the British people, because, in comparison with Germany, Britain was not prepared for Hitler's all-encompassing war machine.

Poland fell in just twenty-eight days. Despite its every effort to thwart a German

onslaught, it was ill prepared against a superior enemy that utilised its infantry, tanks, artillery and air force quickly to stamp out any resistance. At the outbreak of the Second World War, Fighter Command was comprised of thirty-nine squadrons – realistically an insufficient number to defeat a far better equipped and more experienced German air force. By this time the Luftwaffe had already tested its aircraft in combat and developed its bomber and fighter tactics, not only during the invasion of Poland but also during the Spanish Civil War, where many

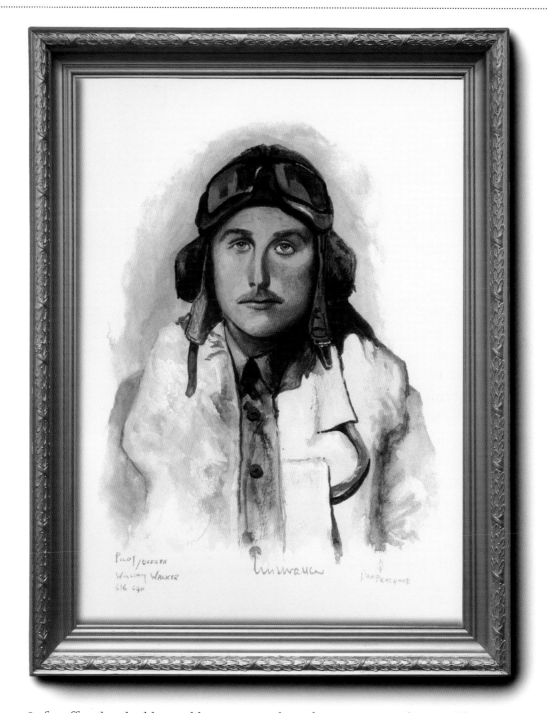

Luftwaffe pilots had been able to gain vital combat experience that would ensure their confidence against the inexperienced RAF pilots.

For Britain it was a desperate time, and preparations were quickly under way. Shelters were built, pillboxes were constructed, and the training of ground crews and pilots accelerated. Right from the outset, a wave of initial urgency and panic swept across Britain, which caused a number of false alarms and accidents to occur. The most serious of these happened on 6 September 1939, when search-

light batteries reported a hostile aircraft in the region of Essex. In response, Hurricanes of No. 56 Squadron were ordered to intercept, but they were then mistakenly reported as a large enemy formation by an Essex radar station, and Spitfires of No. 74 Squadron were scrambled from Hornchurch. As a result of terrible communication and misidentification, the squadrons were vectored on to each other, and two reserve Hurricanes of No. 56 Squadron were shot down by two Spitfires of No. 74 Squadron's Yellow Section. Tragically, Pilot Officer Montague Hulton-Harrop was killed in the incident, now peculiarly known as 'The Battle of Barking Creek'.

In the south of Britain the following months would pass without incident for many of Fighter Command's pilots. Other than flying coastal and convoy patrols, they still had no engagement with any hostile invaders. This lull before the storm began to be referred to as the 'phoney war'. In France however, a small number of pilots had been sent to reinforce the military as part of the Advanced Air Striking Force. These young British fighter pilots soon came spinner to spinner with Hermann Goering's Luftwaffe and finally got a taste of the action.

On 10 May 1940, Winston Churchill became Britain's Prime Minister, while Germany was continuing its devastating sweep through the Low Countries. The

situation was dismally bleak. A couple of days after Churchill's new appointment he visited France and saw the country's desperate predicament at first hand. Churchill then sent a telegram to Fighter Command's Air Chief Marshall Hugh Dowding to deploy a further six Hurricane squadrons to France to offer urgent support. Openly opposed to the idea, Dowding challenged the request by expressing his concerns to the Air Ministry. Britain was already under-equipped, so losing more aircraft in the defence of a crumbling country was seemingly unwise. Dowding knew that if Britain was to defend itself against Germany, then it would need every single aircraft and pilot it could muster. A few days later Churchill ruled that no more squadrons should be sent abroad. Dowding's foresight would prove invaluable.

With France's imminent collapse looming, the battle-damaged Hurricanes and weary pilots began to return to Britain.

Between 27 May and 4 June 1940, the evacuation of Dunkirk was under way. While the stranded Allied troops were being rescued by an incredible number of sea vessels of all shapes and sizes, Spitfire and Hurricane squadrons flew constant patrols high above the smoky beaches, where they finally duelled with the

Luftwaffe. Others were now learning what a select few had learned in France. Aerial warfare was excruciating on the nerves, it was violent, exhausting and bloody. The evacuation of Dunkirk was a miraculous event. Approximately 338,000 men had safely escaped annihilation or capture, despite being cut off by the German army and suffering exposure to aerial bombardments. In a speech given to the House of Commons on 18 June 1940, Churchill declared:

...the Battle of France is over. I expect that the Battle of Britain is about to begin. Upon this battle depends the survival of Christian civilisation. Upon it depends our own British life, and the long continuity of our institutions and our Empire. The whole fury and might of the enemy must very soon be turned on us. Hitler knows that he will have to break us in this Island or lose the war. If we can stand up to him, all Europe may be free and the life of the world may move forward into broad, sunlit uplands.

In early July 1940, the Luftwaffe began to breach British airspace by flying reconnaissance operations tasked with photographing airfields and coastal ports. The RAF soon began to meet raids of between thirty and fifty enemy aircraft that were detailed to harass British shipping vessels and coastal targets. Because of these early confrontations between British and German fighter pilots, it can, of course, be argued that the Battle of Britain had already begun. But, despite these early raids, it is thought that Hitler's planned invasion of Britain, codenamed 'Operation Sea Lion', ultimately began on 10 July 1940, when the Luftwaffe launched its first attack en masse over the English Channel. Without air supremacy, it was impossible for a German invasion force to land on British soil. There-fore the Luftwaffe began an intensified attack on shipping convoys and Channel ports. Its main objectives were effectively to close the Channel to British shipping and to clear the sky of the RAF.

A new phase of the Battle of Britain was ushered in on 8 August 1940 when the Luftwaffe altered its tactics. Rather than concentrating its attacks solely on the shipping convoys in the Channel, the Luftwaffe turned its attention on Fighter

Command's airfields in the south and south-east, hoping to destroy the RAF not only in the air but also on the ground. The persistent bombardment of airfields and of the radar stations along the coast of England caused the RAF a great deal of gloom. Pilots, ground crew, aircraft and airfields began to be stretched to the limit.

In the first week of September the first bombs fell on London, officially opening that awful period of the war known as the Blitz. Time after time the Luftwaffe came across the Channel in mass formations, dropping tremendous bomb loads on major cities and airfields. Hitler was hell-

bent on crushing the morale of the British people, but the depleted nation stood

firm in unity and courage in the face of terror and would not be bombed into submission. The fifteenth day of September proved a decisive day. The enemy's large-scale raids were met by resilient RAF squadrons that claimed an incredible amount of enemy aircraft destroyed and damaged. It was clear to both sides involved that the tide of battle was turning in Churchill's favour.

The following month was much the same, with the Luftwaffe relentlessly raiding Britain by day and by night while RAF fighter pilots continued to intercept them, never giving way to German suppression. Finally, on 31 October 1940, there was respite for Britain. It was the quietest day in over four months, with only a small number of enemy aircraft dropping scattered bombs in Scotland and East Anglia. Not a single aircraft from either side was lost in combat. The Battle of Britain was officially over, because the Luftwaffe had failed to rid the sky of the RAF, and Britain was finally secure from invasion.

Such was the battle in which the following experiences occurred.

Battle of Britain
Fighter Defences 1940

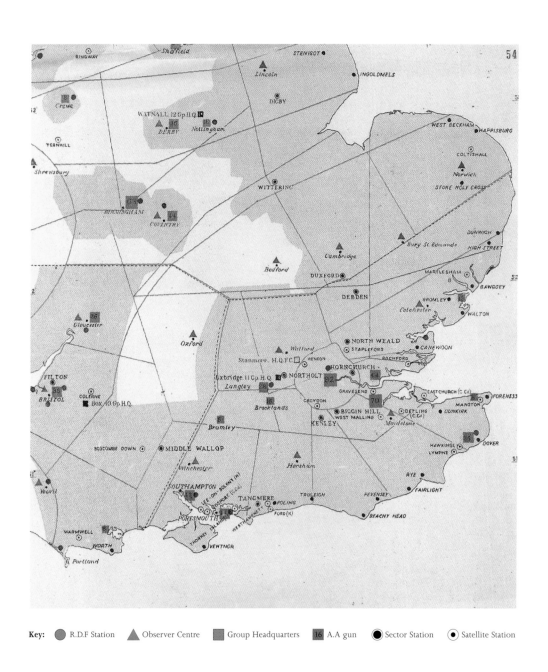

Key: ● R.D.F Station   ▲ Observer Centre   ■ Group Headquarters   16 A.A gun   ◉ Sector Station   ◉ Satellite Station

Portraits of the Few

Group Captain
Billy Drake, DSO, DFC*, DFC (USA)

F/Lt 'Billy' Drake
213 SQN / 421 FLIGHT

Billy Drake

DAVID PRITCHARD

THE UNNERVING THUMPS OF ACK-ACK GUNS BEING fired sounded out across the warm evening air in Rethel, France. Paul Richey hurried through the casualty station, anxious to find the missing pilot of No.1 Squadron. To Richey's great relief, his good friend Billy Drake was alive, although painfully injured. Richey approached the wounded Flying Officer as he lay uncomfortably on his stomach, recovering from the morning's operation. Billy was pleased to see a familiar face and soon explained his predicament.

On 13 May 1940, Drake had been on dawn patrol with five other Hurricanes from his Squadron. Cruising at 22,000 feet in search of enemy aircraft, Drake suddenly began to feel very light-headed. Realising that he had no oxygen, Drake broke away from the Squadron and decided to head back to base. Promptly descending to

As he drifted downwards, Drake heard the 110's engines up above and discovered he was being shot at! Tracer bullets whizzed by, forcing Drake into action.

about 10,000 feet, Drake spotted four Dornier 17 bombers, seemingly unescorted by any fighters. Opening the throttle, the resolute young Hurricane pilot dived in to attack the German bombers. Once positioned at an appropriate firing range, Drake gave a decent burst and set one of the Do 17s ablaze. Suddenly Drake heard a frightening BANG, as his engine burst into flames. A terrible pain shot into Drake's back and leg as he struggled to release himself from the seat harness. A Messerschmitt 110 was hot on his tail, and the scorching flames in front grew alarmingly close. Panic set in. Drake was covered in petrol and glycol, and the cockpit hood was stiff. As Drake forced the hood back, the burning Hurricane turned onto its back, causing the flames to lick upwards and away from him. Drake dropped out of the deadly furnace and desperately pulled the ripcord to his parachute.

As he drifted downwards, Drake heard the 110's engines up above and discovered he was being shot at! Tracer bullets whizzed by, forcing Drake into action. He tried to speed up his descent by tipping air out of the canopy, but the pain in his back soon quelled that idea. Fortunately the Messerschmitt turned away and left the wounded pilot to glide to the ground. Upon landing, the

blond-haired, blue-eyed fighter pilot, dressed in white peacetime overalls, was soon greeted by French peasants bearing scythes and pitchforks. Thinking Drake was a German pilot, the Frenchmen were full of spite. Drake called out 'Pilote anglaise', and once he had convinced them that he was indeed an ally, they embraced him. The pilot was carried to a casualty station, where the French medics gave Drake some morphine and removed the splinters from his back and leg. Lying in the hospital wing feeling lousy, Drake told Richey to ignore the loud bangs outside, even though they were shaking the ward; they had been going on all day. Not long after, the French campaign was over, and No.1 Squadron returned to Tangmere.

Two weeks after Drake's return, he was sent to No. 6 Operational Training Unit at Sutton Bridge. He had chased 109s down under high-tension cables, shared in the destruction of the Luftwaffe's versatile range of bombers, and successfully baled out of a burning Hurricane, so Billy Drake's experience would prove invaluable in preparing new pilots for the coming months of combat over Britain.

One evening in the White Hart pub in Brasted – a popular haunt for fighter pilots during the Battle of Britain – Geoff Wellum remembered seeing a group of people paying a lot of attention to a certain individual he had never seen before. Feeling fairly nonchalant with the whole thing, Wellum asked his pals what the fuss was all about, to which Brian Kingcome responded: 'Now look here "Boy", that is Billy Drake. There stands a real fighter pilot.' When he discovered that the fuss was being made over a Battle of France veteran, Wellum's curiosity soon turned into respect. ■

Pilot Officer
Frank 'Dimmy' Joyce, MBE

PILOT/OFFICER
FRANK (DIMMY) JOYCE
87 SQN
FRANCE 1940

DAVIDPRITCHARD

AT THE OUTBREAK OF THE WAR, NO. 87 SQUADRON was one of those selected to move to France as part of the British Expeditionary Force. It was here that Pilot Officer Frank 'Dimmy' Joyce soon discovered that enemy fighter planes and anti-aircraft guns were not the only dangers a Hurricane fighter pilot could encounter while out on patrol.

On 14 November 1939, No. 87 Squadron received an order to check a report of an enemy reconnaissance aircraft over the English Channel west of Boulogne. Leading a section of three aircraft, Squadron Leader Coope took off with Pilot Officer Joyce and Pilot Officer Dickie Glyde in tow. Once in close formation, the Hurricanes

"...unpleasantly close anti-aircraft shells bursting around us proclaimed that we had intercepted the coast at Ostend."

advanced through thick murky cloud, which broke at 9,000 feet. Squadron Leader Coope then led his section up into the bright sunshine and levelled out at 15,000 feet. Visibility below was poor, and there was no sign of an enemy intruder. To make matters worse there was something wrong with the R/T, so Squadron Leader Coope could communicate only by visual hand signals. After approximately thirty minutes in the patrol area without sighting any enemy aircraft, Squadron Leader Coope signalled to Joyce and Glyde to call it a day.

Having made their descent through cloud, the Hurricanes emerged 2,000 feet over landscape they did not recognise. Wherever they were was certainly not the north-east of France, as they had hoped. Joyce continued the story:

Our leader circled round a small town and I could see his burly, Irwin-jacketed figure perusing a map. Apparently unsuccessful in identifying the place, he took the safe option in these circumstances and turned us onto a north-westerly heading to find the coast. Realising that it would be a long way home I moved the manual mixture control to the WEAK position. After about a quarter of an hour, unpleasantly close anti-aircraft shells bursting around us proclaimed that we had intercepted the coast at Ostend. This was their usual warm warning to any foreign aircraft invading their neutral airspace. (We never knew whether they were poor shots or deliberately aiming to miss us!) Squadron Leader Coope

immediately turned sharply left to escape the fire and headed westerly to follow the coastline. It was now obvious that we had insufficient fuel to reach our base at Lille-Seclin, and I assumed that Coope was heading for the small French naval aerodrome at Dunkirk, some thirty miles distant. Halfway there he suddenly gave a visual 'slowing down' signal, reduced speed to 140 knots, dropped the undercarriage and landed on the beach. This was a complete surprise and I made an orbit to watch Dickie Glyde also land. My fuel gauges indicated that there was just sufficient fuel left, so I continued towards Dunkirk, where I landed six minutes later. The only worry was on my short final approach when I spotted a rather solid earth anti-flood embankment on the aerodrome boundary, which would have finished off the Hurricane if the engine cut suddenly. A sigh of relief when it passed below me! The aerodrome was indeed small and the all-grass ground wet in places, but, thanks to the strong, west wind, I stopped with a few yards to spare.

Later that day, with his Hurricane refuelled, Pilot Officer Joyce took off and flew to Lille-Seclin in the early November dusk. ■

Squadron Leader
Peter Dawbarn

After completing his training in the trusty Tiger Moth, Peter Dawbarn was posted to No. 253 Squadron, stationed at Manston, in November 1939. Cheerfully flying high above Kent with the Hurricane's single pitch propeller spinning happily around in front, Dawbarn felt delighted to be flying in the strong and docile Hawker Hurricane. Such carefree moments would soon become sparse for the enthusiastic young pilot.

In May 1940, Dawbarn joined No. 17 Squadron in France. The hostile skies would sadly take many friends and fellow pilots away from the Squadron. Following a number of ferocious sorties, small relief could be found at the end of the day, when Dawbarn and his pals would visit the local pubs. As a talented pianist, Dawbarn became a popular individual around the mess, and he was often found brightening the mood with his music.

When France fell, the Squadron was withdrawn, and Dawbarn returned to England. Five days into the Battle of

...Dawbarn rapidly began to search for a place to force-land, because he was far too low to bale out.

Britain, Dawbarn was leading a section of three Hurricanes as escort support for a convoy of ships off the coast of Essex. As they returned from their patrol, Dawbarn's engine blew up violently about 20 or so miles away from Debden. While smoke and steam emitted from the damaged engine, Dawbarn rapidly began to search for a place to force-land, because he was far too low to bale out. Among the mass woodlands below he caught sight of a small field and nervously aimed for it. Locking the hood back, tightening his harness straps and turning off the ignition, Dawbarn tensed up as he approached the field with his wheels up. The Hurricane slid across the grass on its belly, Dawbarn gasped as he headed towards a group of fast-approaching trees. Utterly powerless, Dawbarn braced for impact, hoping for the best. As the Hurricane entered the woodland, a large branch found its way into the open cockpit and smashed Dawbarn in the face and head. His eyes instantly closed up and blood began to seep from his wounds. With horrible thoughts of an explosion, Dawbarn wrenched himself out of the Hurricane and tried to feel his way to the edge of the field, where a frightened horse galloped and stomped around, making the tension feel even worse. Fortunately, an air-raid warden had seen the accident happen and rushed towards the injured pilot. The warden took Dawbarn to his home nearby.

With a painful, swollen face, Dawbarn was laid on the cottage floor until an ambulance arrived. He subsequently spent six months in hospital feeling miserable.

After Dawbarn's release from hospital, he returned to Debden, where he spent several weeks on ground duties. One night while on duty in the control tower, Dawbarn spotted an aircraft flying around the airfield flashing its Aldis lamp. When he reported the aircraft over the phone, he was told to let it land, as it was a Vickers Wellington returning from an operation, so he signalled to the bomber to come in. When the aircraft landed and began to turn around, Dawbarn discovered that it was not a Wellington at all – it was a Heinkel 111! With a rush of blood, Dawbarn hurried out of the tower with his flare pistol and fired at the Heinkel, which he instantly regretted, because it lit him up like a Christmas tree, making him an exposed target. Fortunately the Heinkel's guns did not retaliate, but the aircraft turned around and took off again into the night, leaving those at Debden utterly stunned.

Following his time at Debden, Peter Dawbarn was then posted to the Central Flying School, where he trained to be a flying instructor. Once he was qualified, he became an instructor at Burnaston near Derby, flying Miles Magisters. ∎

Wing Commander
John Freeborn, DFC*

PILOT OFFICER
JOHN FREEBORN

RAY PRITCHARD

I T WAS ON THE VERY FIRST DAY OF THE **B**ATTLE OF Britain that Pilot Officer John Connell Freeborn opened No. 74 Squadron's account while on patrol over the Thames Estuary. As Red Leader of A Flight, Freeborn received instructions to offer support to a convoy that had become the target of a Dornier 17 with numerous fighter escorts in tow. Never one to shy away from the action, Freeborn led his section right towards a formation of Bf 109s and soon put the formation leader in his gunsight. He opened fire when he was at a range of approximately 50 yards, an excellent distance to deliver an attack, as he was close enough to watch his bullets slice through the German machine, which could do nothing else but drop out of the sky. There was no time to watch its earthbound descent. Freeborn was turning his attention towards another fighter when he had hurriedly to put his aircraft into a stall turn to evade

On 28 July 1940, the fine Sunday weather was quickly ruined by swarms of Luftwaffe invaders darkening the English skies. To counteract the threat, No. 74 Squadron was scrambled, with instructions to engage the escorting Messerschmitts, while a Hurricane squadron dealt with the bombers.

In no time at all, the Tigers were encompassed by a vast amount of enemy aircraft. Leading Yellow Section, Freeborn received the order from 'Sailor' Malan to draw them off. As Yellow Section peeled away from the main formation, Freeborn's Nos 2 and 3 were shot down in quick succession, leaving him in the middle of thirty-six Bf 109s at 18,000 feet. Almost at once Freeborn caught sight of a 109 pulling out of the circle and instantly pursued it. Turning inside the 109, Freeborn pressed the gun button; after a short burst of gunfire, the 109 exploded into a terrific ball of flame. The overwhelming

Turning inside the 109, Freeborn pressed the gun button; after a short burst of gunfire, the enemy aircraft exploded into a terrific ball of flame.

avenging cannon shells being fired by another 109 on his tail. The situation was alarmingly grave, but it was suddenly broken by the intervention of another Spitfire. Although a welcome sight, the Spitfire's presence was almost as dangerous, because, as well as hitting the 109, its bullets also found Freeborn's aircraft and ultimately forced him down. It had been a hair-raising but success-ful sortie for Freeborn, who was clearly relieved when he made it back to Manston in one piece.

At such an early stage of the war, Freeborn had already begun to show his resilience as a fighter pilot. He had been with No. 74 Squadron, nicknamed the Tigers, since he was just 18 years of age, when the Squadron was flying Gloster Gauntlets at Hornchurch, before being re-equipped with Supermarine Spitfires. Freeborn had already been involved in numerous active patrols with the squadron and had claimed two enemy aircraft as destroyed during the Dunkirk evacuation. Freeborn's summer campaign was just beginning, but it would be a long and arduous one for the young man from Middleton, Yorkshire, for he would fly more operational hours during the Battle of Britain than any other RAF pilot. It was a frightening era for Freeborn, despite his confidence in himself as a pilot. Although fear often crept in before a patrol, Freeborn found that, once he was airborne, it would soon settle down.

odds quickly became apparent, for Freeborn's Spitfire was riddled with cannon shells. As he dived out of the circle towards the sea, Freeborn's reflector sight was hit by the 109s' cannons. Glass shattered everywhere from inside the cockpit, as further cannon shells struck the windscreen. Fortunately for Freeborn, his goggles protected his eyes, and the armour plating behind his seat shielded him from seventeen deadly bullets. Continuing to dive at intense speed, Freeborn was chased down to Brighton pier, where he rolled and twisted to escape his pursuers. Suddenly the Spitfire's engine packed up, but by this time Freeborn had reached an incredible speed of 400 mph and was able to glide back to Manston, where he nervously approached to land.

It was a sorry sight. Freeborn was covered in blood from the exploding glass, and the Spitfire's rudder had been knocked into the main fin, which created a difficult landing. Helplessly, Freeborn held on tight as one of the aircraft's wingtips dug into the grass and tipped the Spitfire up onto its nose, before it fell back down onto its wheels with an uncomfortable bump.

The exhausted fighter pilot was soon dragged from the cockpit by the ground crew, who were alarmed to see blood running from his face, arms, and legs. Freeborn's injuries were not, however, as serious as they appeared to be on the surface. Only an hour later, Freeborn was back in the air leading the Squadron into battle. Such was the pace of war.

Reflecting upon this incident, Freeborn recalled:

That day I couldn't find my flying helmet. I usually kept it on the stick you see, but it wasn't there, so I grabbed Mungo Park's instead. After being clobbered by those German bastards, the helmet was torn to bits and soaked in blood. On returning from the hospital, Mungo said to me 'Freeborn, next time, wear your own bloody helmet!'

Behind every effective squadron during the summer of 1940 was a hard-working and dedicated ground crew that worked tirelessly around the clock to ensure that aircraft were serviceable for their pilots. During the Battle of Britain, Arthur Westerhoff was one of No. 74 Squadron's armourers. He recalled another occasion where John Freeborn almost came unstuck by no fault of his own:

You could be a brilliant pilot and fly your aircraft to perfection, but a tremendous amount of responsibility was with the ground crew to bring that perfection about. The form 700 was the key to it all and before you put your signature to it you were sure all was spot on. One incident comes to mind when we were working on one of No. 74 Squadron Spitfires at Biggin Hill. The ace fighter pilot John Freeborn had returned from a sortie and reported that his guns (four .303mm Browning and two 20mm Hispano cannon) were tremendously out of line. How many German aircraft they had met on the sortie I did not know, but with his armament problem Freeborn had to fight his way out of a difficult situation. The brilliant pilot that he was got himself back to base. His aircraft was put into flying position and his guns checked for correct alignment. One armourer who had worked on Hurricanes suggested that the guns may have been adjusted to meet the requirements of a Hurricane, which flew one degree nose down. The guns were spot on and the fault was found to be with the gunsight in the cockpit, which had to be replaced. That incident could have been the end for John Freeborn, but, as previously stated, his skill as a pilot got him back to base to fight another day.

Arthur continued, offering an interesting insight into the relationship between the pilots and their ground crews during 1940:

No. 74 Squadron was at full stretch from dawn to dusk. Most of our time was spent on the station with little contact with the locals. The pilots that stood out in the Squadron were Malan, Mungo Park, Stephen, Freeborn and Skinner. To say we were friendly with them never happened and most of the talk was shop if they paid a visit to the aircraft. They hung out in or outside their hut and if they were scrambled they dashed out to the kite and were off as quickly as possible with no time for friendly conversation or operational talk. On return the intelligence officer would be there for debriefing. No operational stuff was ever discussed with the ground staff. Our job then was to service the aircraft or re-arm it. We could re-arm a Spitfire in less than seven minutes. Although the emphasis is on friendliness, we never had time for that sort of thing. We were just one big team working together with Malan as the leader. We knew the magnificent job the pilots were doing and we admired them all. There were of course times when the pilots bought a couple of barrels of beer and joined us for a drink to show their appreciation.

The following combat report was written by John Freeborn on the opening day of the Battle of Britain. ∎

Combat Report 10/7/40

```
I was flying as Red Leader, leading 'A'
Flight No. 74 Squadron. I was ordered to
patrol base and then sent to investigate
bombing of a convoy 2 miles east of Deal.
Four bombs were dropped near to the convoy
but no direct hits. I was then ordered to
patrol convoy. I was flying at 12,000 ft
and I saw two aircraft. I then climbed for
height and saw a Do 17 or Do 215 escorted
by 30 Me 109s. I had advantage of height
and ordered 'line astern' and attacked the
Me 109s as they climbed to attack. I
engaged one enemy aircraft and opened fire
at approximately 50 yards. My bullets
entered the enemy aircraft and seemed to
knock it sideways. This aircraft then just
'dropped out of the sky' and was seen to
go down out of control by Observers at
Manston. I then turned to attack another
Me 109. This latter enemy aircraft was
taken off my tail by Red 2. Several other
enemy aircraft got on to my tail. They
were very easy to shake off, but due to
superior numbers I could not shake them
all off. I was finally shot down by enemy
aircraft and I made a successful forced
landing at Manston aerodrome.
```

Flight Lieutenant
Gordon Parkin

PILOT/OFFICER
GORDON PARKIN 501 SQDN

PAUL PRITCHARD

ERIC GORDON PARKIN BEGAN HIS ELEMENTARY flying training at Woodley and was called up to full-time service on 3 September 1939. After converting to Hawker Hurricanes, Pilot Officer Parkin joined No. 501 Squadron in France, but shortly after his posting the Squadron was evacuated and reassembled on British shores. Parkin returned to Britain via Jersey with a pilot officer from Ferndown, Dorset, called Ralph Stidston Don. After catching a ride on a coal boat, they reached Weymouth on 17 June, and then moved on to Croydon to regroup with the Squadron.

On the evening of 31 July 1940, No. 501 Squadron was preparing to return to its base at Gravesend. After a busy day operating from Hawkinge airfield, Gordon Parkin had hoped for a less demanding flight home, but it was just not to be.

When Parkin was unable to start his Hurricane's engine, his Commanding Officer sent word informing him that, if he could not get it started within the next fifteen minutes, then he would have to spend the night at Hawkinge. Fortunately, or so he thought, Parkin managed to get his engine up and running, and he gladly took off for Gravesend in the dim, overcast sky.

On the way back I remember that the engine sounded rather rough, although there [were] no indications in the cockpit that there was something wrong. As I overflew Gravesend the engine hesitated twice and appeared to be losing power. The

"As I overflew Gravesend the engine hesitated twice and appeared to be losing power."

time was only a little after 21.30 hrs but the sky was overcast and the light was beginning to deteriorate; the visibility at one thousand feet was quite reasonable, but became less as I descended.

As Parkin began his final approach to land, he switched on his landing light and hoped that someone on the ground would turn on the boundary lights for just a few minutes to help him land, but unfortunately his hopes were in vain, for the lights did not appear. As the nervous Pilot Officer approached, he saw what he believed to be the airfield boundary pass underneath his wings, but in the bright beam of his landing light he saw rolls of barbed wire! He had undershot the airfield. Parkin's

Hurricane collided with the coiled barbed wire and overturned, leaving the pilot hanging upside down in his straps, with soil littering the cockpit. As a result of this landing accident, Parkin sustained serious injuries and was promptly taken to Gravesend Hospital. This was to end his time with No. 501 Squadron, which had started in France in May 1940.

Parkin was not the only member of the Squadron to come unstuck that evening. Pilot Officer Ralph Don was also returning to Gravesend when his aircraft's engine caught fire. Don was forced to abandon his Hurricane (P3646), and was seriously injured during an awkward landing. His Hurricane crashed and burned out on Lydden Marsh, and Don was admitted to Canterbury Hospital, where he would remain until October.

In early February 1941, Gordon Parkin rejoined No. 501 Squadron and then went on an instructors' course in April. For the rest of the war Parkin continued to instruct new pilots. No. 501 Squadron pilot Bill Green remembers his friendship.

I knew Gordon and his wife Nell very well. He was injured in a crash landing at Gravesend shortly before I rejoined 501 there. I recall going to see him in a local hospital when his head was swathed in bandages. How did I find the time?

In later years our friendship grew through the 501 and Battle of Britain associations' activities. Gordon was one of nature's gentlemen. He and Peter Hairs were great friends. ■

Wing Commander
Wilf Sizer, DFC

F/O WILF SIZER

WILFRED MAX SIZER WAS BORN ON 23 FEBRUARY 1920 in Chelmsford. As a young lad, he had always dreamed of flying aircraft, so, when the time finally arrived in March 1938, he joined the RAF on a short-service commission. Sizer went on to complete his flying training and was initially sent to No. 17 Squadron, but he was then posted to No. 213 Squadron at Wittering in May 1939.

It was 16 May 1940 when Wilf Sizer left for Merville, France, with B Flight, to support other RAF squadrons in their fight against an overwhelming German advance.

On 19 May Sizer was quick off the mark when he succeeded in sharing in the destruction of two Henschel Hs 126s, which the enemy used for spotting and reconnaissance sorties to aid the Wehrmacht's ever-nearing

....

Combat Report 19/5/40

```
Yellow Section consisting of 2 aircraft
were patrolling Tournai - Audenarde with
Red Section. AA bursts were seen below and
flight dived down after it. Red 1 & 2
attacked and I attacked third. By this time
the aircraft was flying very low turning
sharply but with no engine. The other
aircraft attacked it and it fell in a
field. AA fire was experienced from nearby
but no one was hit. Aircraft had swastikas
on side of fuselage and one rear gun.
```

....

columns. The following day, Sizer's Hurricane was ruthlessly set upon by five Bf 109s, which riddled his aircraft with cannon and machine gunfire. With a damaged engine, Sizer managed to glide towards the ground before landing on the Hurricane's belly near

Sizer flew into a cluster of Ju 87s and awakened his guns. His attack put a Ju 87's engine out of action, and Sizer watched as the crew leapt from the damaged Stuka before he climbed away.

La Panne, which was just inside enemy territory. To escape his unfortunate predicament, Sizer swam across a canal and reached friendly territory, where he received

treatment for his facial wounds. After a speedy recovery, Sizer rejoined his squadron after it had been withdrawn from Merville and returned to England. With France lost, it was critical for Britain to be preserved.

No. 213 Squadron had a heavy day of combat on 15 August 1940. Flying with Green Section, Sizer was ambushed by a large group of Bf 110s. Fighting his way out of the attack, he managed to fire a quick burst at a diving 110 and saw pieces fall away from it. The sky was full of opportunity.

At 8,000 feet, Sizer flew into a cluster of Ju 87s and awakened his guns. His attack put a Ju 87's engine out of action, and Sizer watched as the crew leapt from the damaged Stuka before he climbed away.

Sizer soon found himself squirting at another Ju 87 that had pulled up in a stall turn. After some accurate deflection shooting from Sizer, the Stuka dropped out of the air and plunged into the sea. Sizer broke away and soon latched onto a Bf 110. After expending the remainder of his ammunition and seeing no results, he set course for Tangmere. It had been a frantic but victorious day for the young pilot.

An outstanding character, Wilf Sizer naturally acquired the attributes of a fine leader. On one particular occasion when his squadron was scrambled, King George V was visiting the aerodrome. As the hurrying pilots ran out of the dispersal hut's door, Sizer was seen bringing up the rear, brandishing a cricket bat above his head. As Wilf passed the King, he remarked, 'Sorry sir, we have a slight morale problem!' and carried on towards the aircraft waving the bat.

In early October Wilf Sizer succeeded in destroying a Ju 88 with his wingman, over Beachy Head. He was soon after awarded the Distinguished Flying Cross for scoring 7 and 5 shared aerial victories against the Luftwaffe. ∎

Wing Commander
Peter Ayerst, DFC

WING COMMANDER
PETER AYERST

DAVID PRITCHARD

Peter Ayerst

IT HAD BEEN ANOTHER DEMANDING DAY FOR THE instructors at Hawarden. The intense fighting over Britain was taking its toll on Fighter Command's pilots. Losses were heavy and the need for new fighter boys became a desperate cause. Instructor Peter Ayerst had tangled with the Luftwaffe over France and was now performing the essential task of preparing new recruits for action.

The warm evening air soothed the relaxing instructors as they enjoyed a refreshing beer in the marquee. Ground crews were in the process of covering the silent Spitfires when thunderous bangs suddenly pounded in the distance with terrifying force. The alarmed instructors fled out of the marquee to witness bombs being dropped

observed a white circle, but could not distinguish the centre markings. They came up alongside me flying in the same direction at approximately 300 yards, and I did not then recognise them as Messerschmitt 109s; they passed and climbed above me in 'line astern' formation, and turned away from me, presumably to attack me in the rear. I found it easy to turn inside the enemy aircraft, and noticed at the same time that a further nine machines were approaching me in the distance. At this instant I was within 50 yards of this 'line astern' formation, which incidentally was very ragged.

My obvious course was to head for friendly territory immediately. I dived past and under the formation south-west for the frontier, at the same time skidding. The enemy aircraft followed me for approximately 10 miles into France,

The Spitfire's machine guns pelted the Heinkel's fuselage and damaged an engine, causing the bomber to descend rapidly.

on the training school by a lone bomber. Ayerst and two other instructors set off towards their aircraft, while the ground crew heaved back the covers and fired up their engines.

At approximately 2,000 feet the growling Spitfires intercepted the menace on its second bombing run. Two of the instructors fired accurate bursts into the Heinkel 111, but it continued to press on. Ayerst closed in at 200 yards astern and pressed the gun button. The Spitfire's machine guns pelted the Heinkel's fuselage and damaged an engine, causing the bomber to descend rapidly. Ayerst followed it down and watched the He 111 crash-land onto its belly. The bomber stopped 50 feet short of a farmhouse, and Ayerst climbed away. After setting fire to their beaten aircraft, the surviving German crew were taken prisoner.

The following extract is taken from a report Peter Ayerst wrote as a pilot officer about an interesting skirmish that took place at 14.45 hours on 6 November 1939, after he had received information that an enemy aircraft was in No. 73 Squadron's vicinity.

Flying north-east of Metz I saw in the distance what I took to be my target; having followed it over the frontier to approximately 10 miles east of SAARLAUTERN, I noticed nine aircraft climbing up beneath me in the same direction. On first inspection I mistook these aircraft for Hurricanes, because at a distance on the upper mainplanes and fuselage I

where they were intercepted and attacked by French Morane fighters, and possibly a Curtis. As I was becoming short of petrol I landed at Nancy and owing to bad weather conditions remained there overnight.

It was discovered that a strut on the starboard tailplane was damaged by machine-gun fire. In addition there were three holes in the fabric of the tailplane but not sufficiently serious as to prevent me flying the machine back on the following morning. I noticed that anti-aircraft guns fired a few shells before the engagement.

I found it difficult to recognise the machines immediately as enemy aircraft, because of their resemblance to Hurricanes and Spitfires; they appeared to me to be all black and the under surface was not seen. The Hurricane was superior in speed, and I believe in my dive that they were left a considerable distance behind. ∎

Wing Commander
Bob Doe, DSO, DFC*

THE DAY BOB DOE FELL IN LOVE WITH THE SPITFIRE was one he would never forget. On 20 March 1940, the handsome young man stepped out onto the airfield and watched in awe as a solitary Supermarine Spitfire landed and taxied over to No. 234 Squadron's hanger. With joyous enthusiasm, he walked around the beautiful little aeroplane with his colleagues, absorbing its every feature. After running his hand along the smooth fuselage, he hopped up onto the port wing and climbed into the cockpit. There in the snug little haven Doe felt at home and was soon convinced that the Spitfire had to be the most incredible aircraft in the world. Five days later Doe was flying Spitfire P9365 high above the English countryside and through the clear blue sky. While soaring through the air, the young pilot officer from Reigate, Surrey, thought it a great shame that such a lovely invention would be sent to war. Later that same day Doe was able to fly another Spitfire (N3191) to get used to the aircraft before a rigorous schedule of formation flying and battle climbs with the Squadron. Such practice flights would soon become a luxury.

On 15 August 1940, No. 234 Squadron was scrambled south of Swanage to intercept 200-plus bandits. A surge of anxiety rushed through Doe's stomach as he ran towards his aircraft with the rest of the Squadron. A fact Bob Doe was all too aware of was that he absolutely hated aerobatics even to the extent of flying upside down, so thoughts of being shot out of the sky on his very first encounter with the enemy began unavoidably to creep in. Soon enough his thoughts were drowned out by a powerful Merlin engine cutting into the evening air. After racing across the grass airfield with his section, Doe lifted his aircraft into a daunting sky and climbed heavenwards. Once the Squadron was in formation and at its correct patrol line, the rigorous searching was under way. Sure enough the little black specks in the distance turned out to be enemy aircraft bearing black crosses. High up over Swanage Pilot Officer Doe would be among at least fifty enemy aircraft for the first time. The sky appeared chaotic as aircraft broke away in all directions at great speeds.

Being in a favourable position – slightly behind and above the enemy formation – Doe followed Blue 1, his Commanding Officer, into attack. Picking out a Bf 110 from the armada of machines, Blue 1 opened fire and then broke off, allowing Doe to close in. By now the enemy aircraft was diving towards the sea, and Doe followed it closely, undeterred by the rear gunner's attempts to thwart his attack. Once the Bf 110 was trapped in his reflector sight, Doe gave the aircraft a 7-second squirt from 100 yards. The enemy aircraft had no chance of pulling out of the dive as a stream of bullets washed over its fuselage, making a sound like stones pelting against a tin roof. Doe watched the aircraft collide with the Channel and then pulled back on the control

Squeezing the gun button, he let the eight .303 machine guns loose.

column to climb back into the blue sky. Then out of nowhere another Bf 110 overshot his Spitfire from behind, and Doe had to fix his sights on a new target. It was almost too good to be true, but Doe was not going to complain. Squeezing the gun button, he let the eight .303 machine guns loose and peppered the German aircraft with a hail of bullets. Blue 1 also engaged the 110 and finally put it out of action. To his great surprise and not to mention relief, Bob Doe had shot down two enemy aircraft on his first day of combat without really thinking about what he was doing. The experience was unnerving and exhilarating all at the same time.

Doused in sweat and heavy with exhaustion, Doe safely returned to Middle Wallop and retired to his room early to be alone with his thoughts. He spent a restless night pondering the day's action and began working out what he needed to do in order to stay alive. Haunting fears of freezing up in combat and being guilty of cowardice had dispersed.

....

Combat Report 15.8.40

```
I was Blue 2. Patrolling Swanage at
15,000' was led up behind 50 E.A. Blue 1
attacked 1 Jaguar and then broke away.
I closed in and followed it down until it
hit the water (the rear gunner was firing
all the time until at 1000' he baled out).
In the dive I gave it a 7 sec burst from
100 yards as the fire from the engines
appeared to stop. I broke away upwards
towards a formation of ME 110s (3) which
were diving through a thick haze at about
4500'. Fired rest of ammunition at nearest
aircraft. Pieces flew off it as I broke
away. I saw Blue 1 engage the same aircraft
which caught fire and crashed in the sea.
```
....

The following day broke far too soon, and again No. 234 Squadron was at readiness. The weather was fair and warm over Britain, and the Luftwaffe continued its

The chase was on. Doe opened proceedings with a 2-second burst and followed up with three more of the same.

breach of airspace throughout much of the afternoon. When the evening arrived Bob Doe was again airborne, flying as Blue 3 with a squadron of vigilant Spitfires at 16,000 feet. Some distance away from the south of the Isle of Wight, Doe saw a mass formation of Bf 109s flying at 21,000 feet. The call to attack was issued, and the Squadron climbed to meet them. When he was at the same height as the enemy, Doe spotted seven 109s flying in line astern and heading out towards the sea, but he was rudely disturbed by three 109s diving down at him from each side. Doe took evasive action and turned his aircraft away, but soon found himself on the tail of one of the German fighters. The chase was on. Doe opened proceedings with a 2-second burst and followed up with three more of the same. Smoke was observed trailing out of one of the 109's engines as it turned on its back and went down to sea level; the fight was over. As the 109 submerged in the water below, Doe spotted a Dornier Do 18 sea boat about a mile off in the distance coming north towards the coast. Doe closed his throttle and put the flaps down to reduce his speed. Somewhere around 140–160 mph, Doe opened fire at 200 yards range. The rear gunner was silenced and the rear engine stopped dead. As the Dornier banked to the right-hand side, Doe expended the rest of his ammunition and put the front engine out of use. The Dornier landed on the water and appeared to go down nose first. Tired and totally out of ammunition, Doe could only turn and head for home.

Upon landing back at Middle Wallop, Doe discovered that the rear gunner from the Dornier had put a bullet through his Spitfire's spinner, right in the centre of his propeller. It was a startling sight, but after speaking with his friend Pat Hughes, he realised that the encounter could have been a whole lot worse. During the encounter with the enemy fighters, Hughes had witnessed Doe shooting a 109 down but had saved him from another that Doe had not seen by shooting it off his tail. The news

was sobering for the young pilot officer, but Doe continued to learn from his experiences. The following day he wore a silk scarf instead of a collar and tie to allow himself more freedom and comfort in the cockpit while he was searching his surroundings for the enemy.

On 18 August, the Squadron would tangle yet again with a formation of Messerschmitt 109s over the Isle of Wight on an afternoon sortie. Once the scrap was over, Doe completed the combat report, claiming a 109 as confirmed and another as damaged.

....

Combat Report 18.8.40

```
I was in red section and intercepted an
Me 109 over the Isle of Wight. I chased
it from 12,000 ft to sea level out to sea.
The fifth burst set fire to the engine and
aircraft crashed into the sea.

2. I fired at an Me 109 at 1,000 ft. gave
it two bursts, saw them enter engine from
the quarter. No ammunition left so
returned.
```
....

In such a short period of time Bob Doe was proving to be a formidable fighter pilot. His early successes undoubtedly gave him the confidence he needed to continue to duel with and to destroy enemy aircraft during the Battle of Britain with tremendous fervency. ∎

WING COMMANDER
BOB DOE

DAVIDPRITCHARD

Air Commodore
Pete Brothers, DSO, DFC*

ON 23 MAY 1940, AT AROUND 1300 HOURS, A Blenheim aircraft was carrying out a reconnaissance mission east of Ypres. The weather was dismal, with low cloud and heavy rain. Peter Malam Brothers of No. 32 Squadron's B Flight was escorting the Blenheim when he sighted approximately eighteen Bf 110s and fourteen Bf 109s behind them. He turned his Hurricane in their direction and began to climb desperately for height, but soon lost them in the dense

"My aircraft shuddered and I saw a hail of tracer bullets passing to my left…"

clouds. Brothers turned and circled the area until he noticed a dogfight taking place below between Hurricanes and 109s. At an opportune moment Brothers saw a 109 pull out of the fight, so he dropped down onto his tail and opened fire from 100 yards and closing. Brothers saw pieces of the Messerschmitt break off and followed it down in a steep dive. It was trailing smoke and spluttering oil, until finally the fighter hit the ground. Brothers climbed back up into the air with confirmation of his victory. The sky seemed empty, so he turned his Hurricane and set course for home. The return trip was a cause of anxiety for Brothers because his engine was running very badly, so he climbed high and crossed the Channel with his fingers crossed.

During the busy summer of 1940, Pete Brothers continued to serve with No. 32 Squadron as a Flight Commander stationed at Biggin Hill. This period was extremely intense and difficult for the brave men of Fighter Command, as Luftwaffe invaders persisted in their unrelenting mass attacks on Britain. Reflecting upon one particular incident during this time, Brothers remarked:

Early August 1940, having been tangled up with a large number of unfriendly aircraft in a dogfight from which I had escaped without having had any success, as usual I found myself alone in an empty sky. Carefully searching to make sure some foe was not about to attack me, I spotted a vic formation of five Me 109s above me and wending their way home. This, I thought, is too good to be true; I will climb up behind them and pick them off. As I drew nearer the Me 109 on the right of the vic, it eased away to the right. He has seen me, I thought, and said to myself 'Okay, I'll not be

greedy, I'll be content with having you.' As I closed to firing range, he opened his throttle and pulled up into a steep climb, which I could not follow. My aircraft shuddered and I saw a hail of tracer bullets passing to my left and hitting my left wing followed by the first of the four Me 109s whizzing past, all four having a shot at me as they went. They must have been indifferent shots as they failed to do major damage or hit me. I was very, very frightened but worse was in a furious rage. Here I was, an experienced fighter pilot, falling into such an obvious trap. I was livid with myself and furious that I could be so stupid. I flew back to Biggin Hill still seething with rage and counted the holes in my aircraft and my wooden Rotol propeller.

Despite his Hurricane being the worse for wear, Brothers had lived to fight another day. ∎

The following is a combat report that was written after an engagement over Westham at 1715 hours.

```
Combat Report 16.8.40

I was leading Blue Section, in company
with Red Section, when I sighted approx.
80 Ju 88s escorted by 20 Me 110s. I dived
through the formation of Ju 88s and fired
a short burst at two, with no apparent
success. I was in a poor position, when
I broke away I had to give chase.
I eventually caught up a Me 110 cruising
behind the Ju 88s and fired all my rounds
into him from below and behind. His port
engine was smoking badly and he slowly
turned to port and dived through the
clouds. I followed him down and he hit the
sea about 12 miles due South of Brighton.
```

Group Captain
Allan Wright, DFC*, AFC

F/O ALLAN WRIGHT
92 SQN.

ALLAN RICHARD WRIGHT WAS 19 YEARS OLD WHEN he joined No. 92 Squadron. He was born in Teignmouth, Devon, to Elise and Arthur Wright. As a young boy, Wright was moved around with his family, because his father served in the Royal Flying Corps. It seemed that flying was in his blood. As a young man Wright excelled in his education and was shaping up to be an excellent athlete in most sporting activities. He was a skilled marksman for his school's shooting team and won several prizes for his accuracy. In April 1938 Wright arrived at RAF Cranwell, a highly respected college where students were trained to be permanent officers in the RAF. In October 1939 Wright was commissioned as a pilot officer and posted to No. 92 Squadron, stationed at Tangmere. During 1940 No. 92 Squadron was gaining quite a reputation for its flamboyancy and unorthodox culture. It was a squadron that thrived on living in the moment, its indulgence for late-night parties and its lax dress code befitting RAF officers. Regardless of its unconventional activities, it was unquestionably a crack-shot squadron in the air. It did not take Allan Wright long to settle into squadron life, although he was quite unlike many of his counterparts. He was a mild-mannered, religious young man, thoughtful and modest. He had a great interest in photography and would often find himself taking snaps of his surroundings when he was not on flying duty. Highly regarded by his fellow pilots, despite often being aloof from their late-night activities, Wright was to become an integral part of 92.

Initially the Squadron was equipped with Bristol Blenheims, but in early 1940 these were replaced by Spitfires. Wright, like every other pilot in the Squadron, was thoroughly relieved by the change of aircraft.

On 23 May 1940 twelve Spitfires of No. 92 Squadron were airborne over the French coast. It was their first operational flight and it started in a most terrible way. At around 1130 hours over Dunkirk, the Squadron caught sight of enemy aircraft, but it was already too late for Pilot Officer Pat Learmond. His Spitfire erupted into a ball of fire and dropped out of the sky. It was a difficult introduction to combat for the Squadron and for Allan, who was particularly close friends with Pat. Later in the evening the Squadron would respond by destroying seven Bf 110s with an additional four probables. On this engagement Wright claimed one as destroyed and one as damaged.

During the Battle of Britain, No. 92 Squadron continued to be a thorn in the Luftwaffe's side. Between August and September Allan Wright proved to be a prolific marksman in the air, staking claims on almost every type of aircraft in Goering's arsenal. His first target was an He 111, which he shared with Bill Williams on Wednesday, 14 August, while leading Green Section on an evening patrol. Wright's combat report details the encounter.

....

Combat Report 14.8.40

At 1710 hours Green Section was ordered towards Bristol at 15000 feet. After patrolling at 15000 feet the Section was vectored N.E. at 6000 feet. One Heinkel 111 was sighted just below at 500 feet at 1735 hours near Hullavington. It turned up right into the clouds and I as Green 1 fired a short deflection burst at 400 yards before it disappeared. Flying below cloud I saw it again in the next clear patch and got in another longer burst from below following up into astern, again at 400 yards. Again it disappeared in cloud flying on a course towards Bristol but although I flew below and in cloud I did not see it again. A little return fire was observed at first only.

....

On 29 August 1940, Allan Wright taxied his Spitfire across the small, rough airfield at Bibury, under a moonlit sky, feeling elated with success. After switching off the aircraft's engine, Wright climbed out of his cockpit and made his way towards his colleagues in No. 92 Squadron only to find a bunch of morose-looking pilots. Much to Wright's surprise, what had been a victorious sortie was being greeted by groans and grimaces from his fellow chums.

Flying as Blue 1 on a lone night patrol that evening, Wright had been vectored towards a bandit flying near Bristol. Night flying was no easy task in itself, let alone trying to find a single enemy aircraft in the black night sky. Aside from the lack of visibility, it was next to impossible for a pilot's eyes to adjust to the darkness because of the Spitfire's exhausts flaring out in front of the cockpit. Nevertheless, following orders, Wright had continued his search for the enemy aircraft, until eventually he had begun to hear a German crew chatting away over the R/T. The chatter had increased and grown louder, giving Wright the feeling that he was eerily close to the enemy. Then suddenly, at approximately 20,000 feet, Wright had spotted a Heinkel 111 exposed in the beams of a searchlight battery below. Seizing the opportunity, Wright had manœuvred his aircraft into position and then fired two bursts of ammunition from approximately 250 yards between the 111's engines. During the attack, Wright had been blinded for a few seconds by two bright flashes, which at the time he had thought to be enemy return fire. It had in fact been anti-aircraft fire being launched into the air from below. Although a little too close for comfort, the danger of being hit by ground fire had soon passed when the searchlight beams had lost track of the bandit, leaving Wright to close in on the target from between 100 and 40 yards. With attacks continuing from below and astern, Wright had fought vigorously not to overshoot the Heinkel, while watching his De Wilde ammunition burst into the glowing engines. Finally the 111 had decreased its speed, as each engine was rendered useless by the Spitfire's blazing guns. Wright had witnessed a bright flash of flame as the bandit had descended and then plunged towards the earth. At around 13,000 feet, Wright had broken off and returned to base.

Wright had achieved a marvellous feat for the Squadron, but his elation was quickly quelled by the complaints of his fellow comrades at Bibury. Although the boys of No. 92 Squadron knew this was a superb achievement, they could not help but bemoan it, for, just prior to this engagement, Flight Lieutenant Brian Kingcome had been on the verge of convincing 10 Group that night defence was unproductive, hazardous and a waste of the 92's efforts. The Squadron was extremely keen to get back to the south-east, where the Battle of Britain was still raging and the burden of night flying would be lifted. Unintentionally, Wright's success had foiled Kingcome's case – or so they thought. But a couple of days later the Squadron was posted to Biggin Hill, so Wright was duly let off the hook.

On 11 September Wright would harass yet another He 111. Twenty minutes after taking off from Biggin Hill with the Squadron on an afternoon patrol, Wright became separated from the others. Finding himself alone in a vast sky of dangers, he decided to climb to 25,000 feet and position himself over Croydon. About thirty minutes later Wright saw a large formation of bombers approaching, seemingly unescorted. He performed a head-on and quarter attack at the leading formation, but then dived away as a formation of Me 109s entered the arena. During Wright's descent he noticed one of the bombers breaking away from the leading formation with smoke emitting from one of its engines. After climbing to 20,000 feet towards the sun, Wright turned his aircraft and saw the formation heading towards Dungeness. Unable to catch them, Wright turned his attention to an He 111, which he in turn attacked with three other Spitfires of No. 66 Squadron. The Heinkel could do nothing else but crash on the Dungeness peninsular.

The following combat report was made by Pilot Officer Allan Wright on 19 September 1940, while stationed with No. 92 Squadron at Biggin Hill. ■

....
Combat Report 19.9.40

Red 1 and Red 2 set off at 1222 hours on interception. One Ju. 88 was intercepted at 8000 feet within 5 minutes of take off over Base.

I was Red 1 and both gave chase to the Ju. 88 which dived down to broken clouds at 4000 feet. During the hunt which followed Red 2 gave about 3 bursts before we lost the bandit. I gave about 2 two second bursts from abeam at 400 yards and several short bursts at 300 yards with small deflection. Finally I gave him a good 7 second burst from 250 yards to 75 yards from astern position to full deflection from above. I had then run out of ammunition and followed the aircraft for about 10 minutes. It continued to take evasive action travelling more slowly until I lost it in a large bank of cloud travelling S. from Canterbury at about 1245 hours.

Later the bandit was seen by the Observer Corps passing over Dover travelling S.E. at about 900 feet with smoke pouring from both engines and tail.

After using up all my ammunition I repeatedly called up Biggin Hill for Pipsqueak zero, so that the Controller could have a direct plot of the bomber from my own Pipsqueak, as both Red 2 and Green 1 and 2 were in the air trying to find the bomber. Biggin Hill could not hear me and I later remembered that I had no Pipsqueak crystal as there are insufficient on the Station for the whole Squadron.

Landed Biggin Hill 1300 hours.
....

F/O Allan Wright

Wing Commander
Paul Farnes, DFM

Sgt/Pilot
Paul Farnes
501 sqn 1940

At the end of July 1940, Sergeant Pilot Paul Farnes moved to Gravesend with No. 501 Squadron. By this time the Boscombe-born fighter pilot had already seen action in France, where he had claimed several enemy aircraft as damaged and destroyed. Now amid the chaotic skies of southern England, Farnes was very much involved in a most portentous campaign, which he was proud to be a part of.

On 12 August 1940, at approximately 11.27 a.m., Farnes saw, from the cockpit of his Hurricane, thirty or so Ju 87s dive-bombing naval destroyers in the Channel

Farnes found he was on his own when he reached a swarm of Stukas. As a Ju 87 was diving at a destroyer below, Farnes gave the aircraft a quick deflection burst...

several miles north of North Foreland. As Yellow 3, flying rearguard in the formation, Farnes found he was on his own when he reached a swarm of Stukas. As a Ju 87 was diving at a destroyer below, Farnes gave the aircraft a quick deflection burst and then peeled off after another heading for the French coast. He opened fire for a couple of seconds and silenced the rear gunner before delivering a full beam attack on a third Ju 87 also making its way towards the coast, but the short burst did not appear to cause any damage. Farnes then turned his Hurricane back towards the destroyers and met two more 87s head-on, flying about 500 yards apart. 'I fired at each of them in turn, the two bursts being about 2 seconds each. I noticed in each of these attacks a bright red blotch where the spinner is situated. I took this to be cannon fire; a fair amount of tracer was passing over and above my wings.'

Finally, during this adrenaline-fuelled brawl with the Stukas, the Sergeant Pilot's parting attack put one conclusively out of the fight when he opened fire from dead astern, allowing a 6-second burst to disable the machine. It lurched badly to starboard and was seen by Green 1 to dive into the sea. To avoid being hit by the second Stuka involved in this encounter, Farnes broke off for the coast having fired a total of 2,080 rounds.

The following month Paul Farnes had a noteworthy experience when on an evening patrol near Gatwick aerodrome. While climbing with the Squadron to a height of 20,000 feet, Farnes reached 14,000 feet before he became so cold that he had to break off from the

others. The reason for this was that his hood was jammed open and would not budge, so the freezing cold Sergeant Pilot made his way back down through the evening clouds. On his return to base he sighted a seemingly wounded Ju 88 in a dive trailing a wisp of white smoke. Observing its position, Farnes accelerated towards the bomber and caught it at 4,000 feet. The aircraft turned towards his Hurricane, so Farnes opened fire from slightly head-on and broke away 20 yards behind its tail, turning his aircraft for another pass. Suddenly the 88 was out of sight, but Farnes noticed several vehicles below driving across the aerodrome. When he looked in the direction the vehicles were headed, he saw that the aircraft had crash-landed, so Farnes followed suit and also landed at Gatwick. He was soon informed by eye-witnesses that his attack had caused both of the bomber's engines to catch fire and emit black smoke, which forced it down. ∎

After flying as Green 1 with No. 501 Squadron on a morning patrol, Farnes reported the following:

....

Combat Report 8/11/40

I was on patrol with the Squadron, but owing to one section being ordered to investigate a bandit, I got separated. I continued on patrol with about four or five of No.605 Squadron. When I reached 30,000 feet I saw the enemy aircraft below and went to attack. I endeavoured to attack the middle section of about six aircraft, but was unable to do so. I went for the last section of aircraft and picked out two giving one a deflection shot whilst he was turning. I could see my bullets going all round the cockpit, the enemy aircraft turned on its back and spiralled down. I was certain he was out of control as I must have hit the pilot. I then turned my attention to the second enemy aircraft and gave him the rest of my ammunition at 200 yards ending at 350 yards, the only result was smoke although I could see my bullets hitting him when I first fired.

....

Air Commodore
James Coward, AFC

F/LT
JAMES COWARD
19 SQN

JAMES COWARD WAS BASED AT DUXFORD AERODROME in Cambridgeshire with No. 19 Squadron when he first flew a Supermarine Spitfire. No. 19 was the first squadron to receive the aircraft, so Coward believes he was probably about the fourth person in the RAF to have the pleasure of flying R. J. Mitchell's wonderful invention. Unlike most of his squadron colleagues who were single and lived on site, Coward lived in a house a couple of miles away from Duxford with his wife, Cynthia.

As the sun rose over Britain on the morning of 31 August 1940, a new day of conflict was ushered in. It would be a day of fierce aerial combat resulting in heavy losses on both sides: 70 enemy aircraft were destroyed, with an additional 34 probably destroyed and 33 damaged; the RAF's losses numbered 37 aircraft and 12

As Coward was sucked out of his seat, his parachute got caught on the back of the cockpit, forcing his arms to blow back along the side of the aircraft.

pilots killed or missing. It was on this very morning that Flight Lieutenant James Coward would find himself among the fracas.

Having taken off from Fowlmere Airfield, No. 19 Squadron began to sweep the skies for enemy aircraft, patrolling over Duxford and Debden at approximately 20,000 feet. At around 0830 hours, the Squadron was vectored south to intercept a large formation of enemy aircraft flying at 12,000 feet south of Colchester.

Fifteen minutes later, Flight Lieutenant James Coward, leading Green Section, spotted a formation of Dornier 17s flying in sections of three and promptly called out 'Tally-ho! Bandits ahead' over the R/T. Leading his section into position, Coward latched onto one of the bombers and gave it a short burst, but the attack was costly, as Coward felt a thump in his left leg. As the Spitfire accelerated towards the Dornier 17s in front, Coward glanced down and caught sight of his bare foot resting on the rudder pedal. His guns had ceased firing, and it soon became apparent that the control column had stopped working as well. Suddenly the Spitfire's hood tore off, leaving Coward to believe he had collided with the aircraft, but he soon realised the damage could have been from gunfire, as he was under attack from three rear gunners and quite possibly the front gunners of the enemy

aircraft in the section slightly above and behind, not to mention from the fighter escort above or the ack-ack fire below. Whatever it was that had struck his aircraft had caused considerable damage, forcing Coward to bale out.

The danger was not yet over. As Coward was sucked out of his seat, his parachute got caught on the back of the cockpit, forcing his arms to blow back along the side of the aircraft until, suddenly, he was blown clear of the Spitfire. Coward began to fall in somersaults towards the earth, which caused his mangled foot to twist, inflicting sheer agony upon the injured pilot. Coward pulled the ripcord and began his descent in a figure of eight towards the ground. When he looked down, he could see his blood pulsating out in big squirts and he knew that immediate action was needed if he was going to survive. Coward could not reach his First Aid packet in his breast pocket because the parachute straps were so tight over his uniform, so he took the radio lead from his helmet and tied it around his thigh to reduce the bleeding. Several Spitfires circled overhead as if to offer their encouragement as Coward descended towards a field below.

Upon landing Coward quickly gathered up the parachute and placed it under his injured leg to keep it away from the dirt while a young lad ran towards him with a pitchfork. After a few colourful words, the young lad was soon convinced that Coward was not a German and dashed off to find a doctor. Apart from his damaged leg, Coward was also suffering from burns under his arms and crotch, because of being soaked in petrol. James Coward's leg was later amputated. ■

Flight Lieutenant
Bill Green

PILOT/OFFICER
BILL GREEN 501 SQN

Bill Green.

DESPITE THE LIKELIHOOD OF AN INVASION, I NEVER doubted that we would eventually win.

On 29 August 1940 Sergeant Pilot Bill Green decided to write his wife a letter. Having just spent a brief spell of leave with her, the young pilot penned his love for Bertha, and asked her not to be too anxious or worried about him, because the weather was so miserable that day that flying would surely be out of the question. Moments later No. 501 Squadron was scrambled, and Green found himself dashing towards his Hurricane to join the fight.

The Squadron formatted over the evening cloud and was then vectored to Deal to meet the enemy. At 20,000 feet the Hurricanes orbited the overcast sky looking for 200 Bf 109s that were said to be approaching. Green continues the story:

There we were orbiting vigilantly and vigorously looking at all the sky around us, including the sky behind us, when suddenly there was a crash of falling glass and a gaping hole in my windscreen, slightly larger than a tennis ball. Immediately I was covered with liquid of some sort or other and my stick was just useless, it was connected to nothing, so I realised that the airplane was finished. I'm sure I had my hood back and so I pulled the pin of the Sutton harness. I got as far as taking half the weight on my knees, off the seat, so that I was in the semi-crouch position, then I was out. Either I was sucked out or the airplane blew up, I don't know which. I started to roll forward, my legs were spread-eagled and I frantically grabbed around for the rip-cord and eventually found it and pulled it and I saw something white do two

"...suddenly there was a crash of falling glass and a gaping hole in my windscreen..."

eccentric circles going away from me upwards, almost like seeing a large handkerchief disappear and this had no significance until the main canopy just came straight up between my legs like a roller towel and I, rolling forward, just rolled into this unopened parachute. I realised that the parachute should not have come out as it were between my legs but it should have gone out behind me, so I started to try and push the parachute back between my legs. I remember thinking about my wife who I had seen that morning and I suppose eventually I was seeking my end through my thoughts of her because I remember quite clearly thinking

'I wonder if she will wonder, if I wondered as I was falling what my end was going to be like.' And then I remember thinking 'well she'll realise as I realise that everything will go black and that will be it'. I kept struggling with this parachute until eventually there was a jolt and then a secondary jolt.

In spite of everything Green had been hit by, nothing hit him harder than the sheer silence that struck him as he glided towards the earth in his parachute. Passing trees on one side and electricity cables on the other, Bill Green finally landed to safety. 'I sat there on this sloping field, on top of which there was a farmhouse, and the field was full of thistles and cowpats and there I sat in my stocking feet, having lost my boots, thinking "Oh dear, I've got to go and walk through this field in my bare socks."'

Even though he had been shot down by the enemy, Bill Green did not harbour a personal hatred for his opponents, as might have been assumed. In fact, many pilots at the time concentrated their thoughts on shooting down machines rather than the people inside them. 'I was of course angry at the suffering caused to our people and cities by the German bombing, but deep down I knew that their aircrews were people just like us, doing what was their duty. I knew no hatred towards them and do not to this day.' ∎

Squadron Leader
Gerald 'Stapme' Stapleton,
DFC, DFC (Dutch)

F/O Gerald "Stapme" Stapleton

W. G. Stapleton

DAVID...

It was around **1600 hours on 29 August 1940** when nine Spitfires of No. 603 Squadron were airborne and sweeping the hostile skies for any tell-tale signs of enemy aircraft. Patrolling at 24,000 feet over Rochford, 'Stapme' Stapleton was ordered to Deal with the Squadron.

Just south of Deal, the boys of No. 603 spotted eight Bf 109s bearing down on them, with a further six flying in line astern. Working in pairs, the 109s lunged into action. Following Pilot Officer Read, Stapleton broke off from the Squadron and climbed towards two 109s circling above. Stapleton engaged the second bandit at approximately 150 yards and fired two short bursts at the evading Messerschmitt. The 109 dived out of sight, with smoke trailing from its engine. Stapleton pulled firmly back on the control column and lifted the Spitfire's nose into the sun. On returning to the aerodrome, Stapleton discovered that two of the Squadron's pilots had suffered slight injuries in the action; one had been forced to land at Bossingham and the other limped home relatively intact. The Squadron claimed one 109 destroyed and three probables.

The hard-working ground crews quickly set about refuelling the Spitfires' tanks, reloading the spent gun chambers and attending to any other requirements in preparation for the Squadron's next scramble. It was sooner rather than later.

At 1810 hours that same day Stapleton was again prowling through the air with nine other determined No. 603 Squadron Spitfire pilots, patrolling over Manston at 27,000 feet. Sure enough they were soon in the company of twenty-four 109s circling above. Squadron Leader Denholm led the Squadron into a climbing attack to meet the fighters. The mayhem of combat erupted, with planes and bullets whizzing by in all directions.

Stapleton became separated from the others and climbed into the sun to 30,000 feet. The dashing South African scanned his surroundings and spotted a 109 going into a loop. Stapleton jumped upon the bandit and fired a 5-second deflection burst, which trickled along the German's airframe as the 109 continued to climb. Stapleton watched as the 109 abruptly manoeuvred into a steep dive, trying to make the most of the Messerschmitt's fuel-injection advantage. Stapleton released the Spitfire's guns, firing a long burst from 200 yards closing to 50. Pulling out of the attack, Stapleton returned to a safe height and broke off for base, constantly checking over his shoulder. It had been a hectic day, one of many for Churchill's 'Few'.

Combat Report 29/8/40

When on patrol with 603 Squadron we sighted enemy fighters just south of Deal. P/O Read and myself broke away from the Squadron to engage two Me109s who were circling above us. P/O Read engaged the first and myself the second. After firing short deflection bursts the Me109 which I attacked went straight down out of my sight with smoke issuing from the engine. I then broke away and climbed into the sun.

Two days later Pilot Officer Stapleton reported the following after delivering an attack at 1825 hours north of Southend at 25,000 feet.

Combat Report 31/8/40

When patrolling in line astern with the rest of the Squadron I sighted bomber formation below us on the port. With two other aircraft I climbed into the sun for a favourable position, to make attack on the bombers out of the sun, when 5 Me.109's engaged us.

These Me.109's came out of the bomber formations climbing into the sun. F/O. Carbury engaged 3 Me.109's and I engaged the other 2. These two were flying in tight line astern. After giving the rear one a deflection burst of 3 seconds he pulled vertically upwards with white streams pouring from his engine.

By the end of the Battle of Britain, No. 603 Squadron was credited to be the top-scoring squadron in the RAF – of which Stapme Stapleton was always very proud. ■

Flight Lieutenant
William Walker

KENLEY AERODROME WAS A SORRY SIGHT FOR No. 616 Squadron when they arrived at their new station in August 1940. Prior bombing attacks had left a considerable amount of damage to the airfield, its buildings and hangars, but for No. 616 Squadron worse was to follow. In the short space of eight days, the squadron lost five pilots killed or missing and an additional five others were wounded. On 26 August Pilot Officer William Walker would also be numbered among the injured.

At approximately 1000 hours, Yellow Section, consisting of Pilot Officer Walker, Sergeant Ridley and Flying Officer 'Teddy' St Aubyn, was scrambled to patrol Dover/Dungeness at 20,000 feet. After about half an hour of prowling the seemingly placid sky, the three Spitfires were suddenly bounced by a squadron of Messerschmitt 109s. In spite of being vastly out-numbered, Yellow Section swiftly got to work and began turning their aircraft around the blue arena. Selecting one of the enemy fighters, Walker banked his Spitfire towards a 109 but was instantly raked by a hail of bullets from behind. A sudden pain in Walker's leg confirmed the peril. Not only had he been wounded but the aircraft's controls were out of action. There was only one thing for it. The tension mounted as the injured Pilot Officer

…Walker banked his Spitfire towards a 109 but was instantly raked by a hail of bullets from behind. A sudden pain in Walker's leg confirmed the peril.

hurriedly undid his straps and heaved back the Spitfire's hood. As Walker tried to evacuate the cockpit, he was pulled back by his helmet, which was still plugged into the radio. Once the helmet had been removed, the young fighter pilot was free to fall out of the aircraft and drop towards the large cumulus clouds below.

Once through the fluffy clouds, Walker became slightly concerned to see the uninviting Channel staring up at him. He decided to remove his flying boots and musingly watched as they spiralled down towards 'the drink' for what seemed like an age. As Walker hung wounded in his parachute, he was not to know that the rest of Yellow Section had also suffered at the 109s' guns. Flying Officer St Aubyn had been badly burnt when his Spitfire caught fire and Sergeant Ridley had sadly been killed.

As expected, the sea was cold and harsh as Walker plunged into its depths. He quickly detached his parachute. Floating in his Mae West, Walker caught sight of land in the distance, but was unsure if it was England or France. Soon enough, his alert blue eyes spotted the wreckage of a boat about 200 yards away from his position and he slowly swam towards it. Feeling utterly exhausted, Walker climbed onto the boat wreck and held on for dear life, shivering, for about half an hour, until he was eventually picked up by two Englishmen in a fishing boat.

Much later, when Pilot Officer Walker regained consciousness, he was greeted by a surgeon sitting by his bed. The surgeon handed Walker a bullet and told him that, as he had prised open his ankle to extract the bullet, it had shot out and hit the ceiling of the operating theatre.

Today, at 97 years of age, William is still in possession of that very same bullet. ■

Air Commodore
John Ellacombe, DFC*, CB

PILOT/OFFICER
JOHN ELLACOMBE

DAVID PRITCHARD

N EXPLOSION SOUNDED AS A SINGLE BULLET PELTED into the Hurricane's spinner, putting Pilot Officer John Ellacombe in a tense and difficult position. His engine was damaged and there was only one thing for it – he had to get the aircraft down. The fear of being strafed in his parachute by lurking bandits kept the young man pinned to his seat while he looked around for somewhere to force-land. This was not how he had hoped the patrol would turn out.

It was 30 August 1940. The pilots of No. 151 Squadron had embarked on several patrols throughout the morning against the Luftwaffe, but it was later in the day that Pilot Officer Ellacombe got mixed up in the action.

After breaking through cloud, No. 151 Squadron was bounced by an escort of Messerschmitt 109s. To evade their cannons, Pilot Officer Ellacombe put his Hurricane into a tight turn and soon became separated from his

Electing for a head-on attack, Ellacombe braced himself and closed to 2,000 yards before giving the leader a 3–4 second burst of ammunition.

squadron and the German fighter planes. The lone pilot searched his surroundings, seeing nothing but the empty evening sky, until a voice over the R/T alerted him of a large bomber formation heading in the direction of his base airfield 'Bengal'. With keen eyes, Ellacombe soon spotted twelve Heinkel 111s approximately 6 miles away and raced towards them. Electing for a head-on attack, Ellacombe braced himself and closed to 2,000 yards before giving the leader a 3–4-second burst of ammunition. He witnessed hits to both its engines and saw the Heinkel's Perspex break off, before he managed to duck his Hurricane underneath the approaching bomber. It was then that his engine blew up under return fire. Ellacombe managed to win control of his aircraft and sighted a large field in which to put down.

No sooner had the Pilot Officer dismounted from his machine with a sigh of relief and placed his feet on solid ground than he was set upon by an irate man brandishing a pitchfork while shouting threats at the 'German' fighter pilot. Ellacombe raced around his slumbering Hurricane to escape his attacker until he was fortunately rescued by soldiers from an anti-aircraft battery unit that was stationed nearby. After the situation had been

defused, the group watched Ellacombe's damaged Heinkel crash in the adjacent field. Ellacombe was advised not to investigate the wreckage because the sight of the crew might have been distressing. Instead he sat down and knocked back a few pints of draught cider until a van arrived and took him back to North Weald.

Back at North Weald, Ellacombe found his station commander, Victor Beamish, in the bar. With no time to waste, Beamish instructed Ellacombe to find another Hurricane and join him as his No. 2 for the next raid. Ellacombe, drunk with cider, told the station commander that, because of his current state, he probably ought not to fly. When he realised that Ellacombe was dizzy with cider, Beamish agreed. ∎

The following combat report was written by John Ellacombe after attacking enemy aircraft over the west and south-west of Dover at around 1530 hours with Blue Section.

Combat Report 15/08/1940

Nine Hurricanes of 151 Squadron were patrolling at about 18000 when we were attacked by Me 109's. I chased one who had unsuccessfully quarter attacked the leading Hurricane. I fired my first burst at 400 yards, and closed to 200. After firing about 3 bursts I got a 5 second burst in a turn, after which black smoke issued from one 109 and he rolled over on his back, diving. I finished my ammunition at 100 yards when large volumes of black smoke issued. As I was over the French coast I turned back leaving the 109 diving vertically towards the sea. My wireless aerial damaged.

Squadron Leader
Nigel Rose

PILOT OFFICER
NIGEL ROSE
602 SQN.

AFTER COMPLETING HIS TRAINING, PILOT OFFICER Nigel Rose was posted to No. 602 'City of Glasgow' Fighter Squadron, stationed at Drem in East Lothian. The new recruit described the camp as small but pleasant, and soon found the officers to be extremely warm and helpful. But perhaps the most exciting part about the posting was that he would be flying Spitfires! Throughout his time in a fighter squadron, Rose sent regular letters to his parents, and, as a collection, they give some wonderful insights into those trying days over Britain.

In a letter to his parents dated 26 August 1940 Nigel wrote:

Dear Mum and Dad,

Two patrols yesterday, one at 22,000 ft for 20 minutes which didn't have any results, and then in the evening the squadron was ordered off to patrol the Dorset coast at

"The Controller did his job well and brought us slap into a whirling mass of 109s and 110s, and in no time at all it was a free-for-all scrap."

20,000 ft together with a squadron of Hurricanes. The Controller did his job well and brought us slap into a whirling mass of 109s and 110s, and in no time at all it was a free-for-all scrap. I left the 109s alone because I was a bit afraid of going for a Hurricane by mistake, but I got two or three at the 110s at reasonably short range. The last one went down in very similar circs to the one of last Friday week, except this time there was blue-white smoke pouring from his port engine. I followed him down in a dive as far as I could, but had to pull out when I had about 420 mph on the clock (at 12,000 ft this is about 520 true air speed) and I lost sight of him, As I flattened out and turned there was a vivid red explosion on the ground more or less in the direction in which he had been diving, and I assumed that this was the 110. Actually I oughtn't to claim this, but I feel so certain that between my two little efforts I must have got at least one that I'm calling it destroyed.

The squadron's claiming 12 for yesterday's scrap. On my way back I found the top cover to No. 1 Port gun was missing — it must have blown off in the dive. My fuel tank gauge let me down, giving a reading of 18 gallons when I was still at Bournemouth, and 12 gallons when I was crossing Southampton Water, so I assumed my tank was punctured,

and landed at Hamble to see what had happened.

As it turned out, it was only a faulty gauge, and I had plenty of fuel left. When they had given me a new gun cover I returned here.

You must excuse this sudden rush into print, but it's a very good safety-valve to the pent-up excitement to be able to sit down and write short notes about the action.

Incidentally two of our chaps baled out and both are safe - so, touch wood, the squadron is still intact in its personnel, although we've lost quite a lot of Spits altogether.

Hope to find a letter from you today.

Love, as always

Nigel

I hope the London raids have kept well clear.

On 29 October, Rose, comprising part of No. 602 Squadron's A Flight, clashed with the enemy in the region of Biggin Hill, Maidstone. After expending 2,240 rounds of ammunition, he claimed a Messerschmitt 109 as a 'probable'. ∎

....

```
Combat Report 29.10.40

I was Yellow 2, flying in the third
section of 11 aircraft. I saw A/A fire
at 9 o'clock and this drew my attention
to about 50-60 bandits flying south in
two large masses. I followed Yellow 1
into attack and did a quarter stern attack
on one Me. 109 which gave out volumes of
white smoke. E/A turned downwards, and
following another burst, cowlings or
cockpit cover came off. E/A was last seen
diving steeply with white vapour still
streaming. Yellow 3 saw bits of this E/A
falling off, and thick white trail.
```

....

Flight Lieutenant
Richard Jones

Pilot Officer
Richard Jones
64 and 19 Sqn.

David Pritchard

I T WAS IN 1938 AT WOODLEY THAT RICHARD JONES nervously approached a Miles Magister aircraft for the first time. As the charming fighter pilot sat himself down into the cockpit, his eyes caught sight of some unexpected and most discomforting writing on the dashboard. There in red paint were the words 'Note – This A/C will not come out of a spin. Repeat – This A/C will not come out of a spin.' Jones took a deep breath and prepared for his first take-off, despite the demoralising warning and thumping in his chest. As good fortune would have it, Jones survived his first flight in the Magister and went on to complete his training at No. 8 E&RFTS before converting to North American Harvards at Tern Hill.

After a conversion course on Spitfires, Jones was posted to No. 64 Squadron stationed at Kenley. Feeling slightly green, Jones was relieved to find the senior pilots extremely helpful in showing the new recruits the ropes. As he explained:

When off duty the senior experienced pilots used to dogfight with us to give us confidence in the aircraft and to be capable of meeting the enemy in all conditions. Our C/O at the time was Squadron Leader Donald MacDonnell, who called us his chicks and immediately made us feel at home with the station. Squadron Leader MacDonnell was a first class gentleman, an excellent pilot and leader. He had full respect from us all.

In August 1940, when the aerial battles over Britain were heavily under way, Richard Jones recalled one particular occasion when the Squadron was at readiness at Hawkinge. The aerodrome was attacked by low-flying Messerschmitt 109s. Jones remarks:

As it was a low level attack we had no warning. We immediately took to the air but unfortunately my aircraft's engine would not start, so I and others made a dive for the airfield shelter, which was not capable of meeting our numbers. I remember being pushed in the rear by those behind and pushed out! Some ran around the front again and the same thing happened three or four times. At the time it was not funny, but looking back it was quite unusual and amusing.

Jones, like many, if not all other pilots, quickly discovered that readiness was an intolerable experience:

When in the crew room waiting at readiness to take off, the instructions were given to us by phone to get airborne with no delay. This used to happen from sitting down to airborne in approximately 3 minutes, but the telephone in those days proved to be the most hated instrument, because it usually brought bad news.

Although the coming months would prove intensely difficult and often gloomy for the boys of No. 64 Squadron, Jones was able to find solace against the dark backdrop of war in his relationship with Elizabeth. The smitten couple married in November 1940, with Elizabeth choosing to ignore her parents' concerns that she would probably end up a young widow. Alas, such was the case for many women during the war against Hitler. ∎

The following combat report was written by Richard Jones after he, with Yellow Section, engaged the enemy.

. . . .

Combat Report 16.8.40

I was Yellow 2. when we were scrambled up to Angels 20, climbing through clouds at Angels 19. We sighted about 40 Heinkels and a big formation of ME. 109's 6000 feet above the enemy bombers. We were ordered into line astern, Yellow 1. Did beam attack on No. 3 of enemy Vic. of 3 going South, I followed up and also did a Beam attack, giving a long burst, I closed to 100 yards and then broke off the attack. Yellow 1. then did another Beam attack and I followed up with a No. 2. attack giving long bursts of about 8 secs. closing to 150 yards. As I broke away I saw an Enemy aircraft emitting black smoke and breaking away from Vic.

. . . .

Flight Lieutenant
Keith Lawrence, DFC

PILOT OFFICER
KEITH ASHLEY LAWRENCE DFC
234 AND 603 SQNS.
NEW ZEALAND

Keith Lawrence

DAVID PRITCHARD

ON 8 JULY 1940 NEWLY RE-FORMED SQUADRON No. 234 scored its first victory of the Battle of Britain, when a section of Spitfires gunned a Junkers Ju 88 out of the sky. Sharing in the destruction of the Ju 88 was New Zealander Keith Lawrence, flying as Blue 2 in B Flight.

The Squadron sighted enemy aircraft diving through cloud during an evening convoy patrol over the Channel. Turning immediately to intercept, Lawrence joined his section in attacking a Ju 88 that was approximately 4 miles away from the convoy below. When in range of about 300 yards, the New Zealander pressed the gun button and fired six bursts, expending all of his ammunition before breaking away and above the bomber.

Four days later, Lawrence once again encountered another Ju 88 over St Eval, as an extract from his combat report explains:

....

When blue section was ordered off I took off as blue 2, some seconds after blue 1. As soon as I was airborne I turned and looked back seeing the EA behind me on a course almost parallel to my own. I immediately turned towards the EA and climbed steeply, closing to about 275 yds before opening fire with a burst of 1 sec. before EA disappeared in cloud.

....

Later, on 24 August, No. 234 Squadron attacked a large number of Bf 110s flying at 16,000 feet near the Isle of Wight, at approximately 1630 hours. After being separated from Green Section, Lawrence attacked a 110, firing a lengthy burst of ammunition, which caused substantial damage to the aircraft's engine.

Lawrence continued to gain the advantage over his adversaries until 26 November, when he was shot down by Bf 109s over Ramsgate, during a weather reconnaissance sortie. The lethal attack caused his Spitfire to fall apart in the air, but he managed to open his parachute before landing in the sea. Lawrence burst a dye sachet into the water, which attracted a minesweeper, that pulled him to safety. Lawrence was taken to Ramsgate and admitted to hospital with a broken leg and a dislocated arm.

Reflecting upon his time during 1940, Lawrence recalls:

No. 234 Squadron was stationed at RAF Middle Wallop from August until 10 September 1940, engaged in countering Luftwaffe raids over Hampshire, Sussex and Kent. I took part in twenty-one 'scrambles' during this time. The Squadron had numerous successes but also lost eighteen Spitfires and on 7 September our CO, Squadron Leader O'Brien, and B Flight commander, Flight Lieutenant Pat Hughes, were killed in action over Kent in the same engagement. Three days later No. 234 Squadron returned to RAF St Eval, while I was posted to RAF Hornchurch in Essex, to continue flying in action with No. 603 Squadron. In November 1940 I was shot down and injured and remained in hospital for one year, until I was able to take a Spitfire refresher course and return to operational flying with No. 185 Squadron in Malta. ■

The following combat report was recorded after Keith Lawrence had engaged the enemy as part of Green Section.

....

Combat Report 24.8.40

As Green 1 I was in the rear of the squadron formation and about 1,000 ft below. I saw A.A. fire over Portsmouth straight ahead of the squadron formation then saw approx. 70 A/C heading out to sea. Not seeing G 2 and 3 beside me I immediately turned towards E/A opening fire at 200 yds. approx. closing to 50 yds. I opened fire with deflection from the rear and swung round to almost astern. As I closed in I saw black smoke come from the starboard engine. I then broke away below. Length of burst approx 8 secs.

....

Flight Lieutenant
Mike Croskell

Sgt Mike Croskell
213 Sqdn.
Mike Croskell.

David Pritchard

ON 29 MAY 1940 EIGHT HURRICANES FROM No. 213 Squadron were flying top cover to twelve Defiants on the prowl for German bombers over the black, smoky beaches of Dunkirk. Spotting six Heinkel 111s flying south at 17,000 feet, Sergeant Mike Croskell began to climb towards the bombers with the Squadron. Unable to maintain his position as Red 3, he pulled out because of engine trouble. After recovering his Hurricane, Croskell ran into a formation of thirty Ju 87s about to bomb Dunkirk harbour. Croskell dived after one and gave it a solid burst. The Stuka dropped towards the sea with smoke trailing from its engine. Croskell was unable to watch the Stuka's fate, as he was bounced by a Messerschmitt 109. After some tight turning, Croskell shook off his chaser.

· ·

Combat Report 29.5.40

```
The squadron was patrolling Dunkirk at
3000 ft approx. with No. 264 Squadron,
when 6 enemy bombers of the HE 111 class
were sighted about 4000 ft above us. The
squadron climbed to attack same but I was
unable to do so owing to a faulty engine.
Shortly after I sighted about 30 JU 87s
about to attack Dunkirk harbour. I followed
one of the dive bombers down and attacked
him as he pulled out of the dive. He
immediately turned over on his back and
dived for the sea and smoke commenced to
come from his engine. I did not see him go
into the sea as I was immediately attacked
by a ME 109 which I had great difficulty
in evading.
```

· ·

But the ordeal with the 109s was to continue over the following months. In August, over Britain, Croskell watched a German crew bale out of a blazing Ju 88 after being intercepted by No. 213 Squadron. He soon regretted his mistake, as five Bf 109s swooped down onto his tail. The terrifying situation caused the Yorkshireman to throw the Hurricane into a tight turn, with desperate hopes of losing the fighters. Continuing the turn, Croskell latched onto the tail of a 109 and blasted it out of the sky.

But the following month, he was not as fortunate. Reflecting upon the events of 15 September, Croskell remembers: 'It was a busy day up there. I was twenty one, plus two days. The squadron steamed into a forma-

The Hurricane's cockpit exploded with cannon shells and Croskell was hit in the head, shoulder, and left foot and in the back of his knee.

tion of bombers head on.' Passing through the bombers, the Flight Commander turned sharply, forcing Croskell to cut inside and duck underneath him. Separated from his section, Croskell headed towards a Dornier 17 flying below. 'The snag was, I didn't check my rear view mirror and I ended up with two 109s on my tail.'

The Hurricane's cockpit exploded with cannon shells, and Croskell was hit in the head, shoulder, and left foot and in the back of his knee. Part of a cannon shell had caused his canopy to jam, so he had to stand on his seat and heave it back with great effort. By now Croskell was at a dangerously low altitude, but he decided to bale out. As he fell through the air, he heard the Hurricane explode above him, and he feared it would come down on top of him. Mercifully his parachute opened just in time to break his fall, and Croskell ended up in a grove of young trees, where he was rescued by a nearby anti-aircraft crew.

After a speedy recovery, Croskell returned to the front line. Attacking a defensive circle of Messerschmitt 110s from the outside, Croskell ignored the return fire from rear gunners and succeeded in shooting one down. This time, Croskell learned from past mistakes. 'Having congratulated myself on getting one of the bastards, I looked into the mirror and saw two 109s behind me. I pulled up into top cloud and lost them. It must have been the only cloud in the sky, during the summer of 1940.'

Part of the cannon shell that hit Croskell's head in September 1940 can still be felt today. ■

Wing Commander
George 'Grumpy' Unwin,
DSO, DFM*

'FLASH'
19 SQUADRON

FLIGHT
SERGEANT
GEORGE 'GRUMPY' UNWIN

FLIGHT SERGEANT GEORGE 'GRUMPY' UNWIN WAS the absolute opposite of what his nickname implied. In the middle of the night Douglas Bader was making an awful screeching noise as he filed his damaged prosthetic leg. Unwin complained to Bader that he could not sleep and to take his leg somewhere else, to which Bader retorted, 'Oh shut up Grumpy!' and the name stuck from then on.

On 16 August 1940, Unwin's beautiful Alsatian dog, Flash, looked hopefully across the Duxford airfield waiting for his loyal master to return from the day's patrol.

Returning from Coltishall at 1715 hours, No. 19 Squadron's A Flight received orders to investigate a large

Flying as Red 3, Unwin stormed into the bombers with his section but was quickly thwarted by the protective Bf 110.

raid building up southwards above cloud. The seven Spitfires rose to 15,000 feet and searched the area for the tiny black specks of the enemy. Brian Lane led the Flight down to 12,000 feet and, twenty minutes later, 150 bombers with escort fighters were sighted. Flying as Red 3, Unwin stormed into the bombers with his section but was quickly thwarted by the protective Bf 110s. Unwin fired a short burst at one of the fighters, causing it to half roll and dive almost vertically towards the ground. As usual there was not time to confirm the success, because he was instantly attacked by another Bf 110. Unwin promptly jerked the Spitfire to one side and proficiently turned inside the 110. At close range Unwin pressed the gun button to find that the starboard cannon was jammed. With only the port wing's cannon blazing, Unwin hit the 110 and saw bits fly off the descending Messerschmitt, including its tail. Unwin followed it down through cloud to find what he thought to be his attacker immersed in the cruel sea below. Unwin veered off for Duxford, where Flash would surely be waiting. Out of the seven Spitfires, six of them had cannon stoppages on this action, with Flight Lieutenant Lane's being among the first.

In his book *Spitfire*, Brian Lane commented: 'Grumpy with some 109s always reminded me of a terrier among rats!' The action of 15 September 1940 would demonstrate his reasoning. It was a Sunday, and the weather was clear, with occasional patches of cloud. In the early morning hours, Radar systems and the Observation Corps had monitored enemy activity probing the English coasts. The mass build-up of Luftwaffe aircraft was so huge that by midday twenty RAF squadrons were airborne, including the Duxford Wing. Unwin flying again as Red 3 was in the furnace of the day's battle. Diving to intercept some Dornier 17s over London, the Wing was bounced by yellow-nosed Bf 109s. Unwin engaged one of the escorts and gave it a 6-second burst. The pilot managed to bale out as the 109 went down in flames, but his parachute failed to open.

Later in the afternoon, the Squadron was mixing it up with hundreds of enemy aircraft screaming about the skies. At 25,000 feet Unwin caught two 109s from behind and unleashed his cannons. One burst into flames and went into a steep dive and moments later the second 109 caught fire and dropped into the sea. ∎

The following combat report details an action involving George Unwin on the opening day of August 1940.

....

Combat Report 1/8/40

I was Red 3 with F/Lt. Lane, along the coast, about 2 to 3 miles N.E. of Dunkirk 12 E/A were sighted at 4000 feet. We formed line astern and engaged the enemy. They formed line astern and used evasive action by turning. The aircraft looked like Me. Jaguars. I climbed underneath one and gave a burst approx. 5 secs. at 150-100 yds. range. The aircraft blew up over my head. I then chased another who turned and climbed as I got within range. I gave him a long burst, and his starboard engine then stopped and threw out oil and smoke. I carried on firing until about 100 yards, and then dived under him to avoid collision. I looked around for a while for more aircraft but could only see Spitfires. Being almost out of ammunition I returned home. Practically no return fire was experienced. Aircraft were fast. I had to use 12 Boost to catch them. No. of rounds fired - 300.

....

Squadron Leader
Geoffrey Wellum, DFC

FLYING OFFICER

GEOFFREY WELLUM WAS BORN ON 14 AUGUST 1921 in Walthamstow, London. He joined the RAF on a Short Service Commission and began his training flying Tiger Moths at Desford in Leicestershire in July 1939. Wellum then moved to No. 6 FTS Little Rissington in Gloustershire to fly Harvards. After successfully completing his training, Wellum was marked as an 'above-average' pilot and was posted to No. 92 Squadron stationed at Northolt. On his arrival Wellum was soon taken into the mess, where he was introduced to pilots such as Pat Learmond, who was famed to be the

Wellum listened fondly to the familiar sound of awakening Spitfires. The ever dependable fitters were busy warming up the Merlin engines, while sleepy pilots prepared for squadron readiness.

best aerobatic pilot in 92, and Allan Wright, a young man who appeared to be very much in control of himself. At this time Wellum was just 18 years and 9 months of age and would soon become known as 'Boy' among his fellow pilots.

As dawn broke over the airfield at Biggin Hill on 11 September 1940, 'Boy' Wellum listened fondly to the familiar sound of awakening Spitfires. The ever dependable fitters were busy warming up the Merlin engines, while sleepy pilots prepared for squadron readiness. Cockpit checks were completed and the awful spell of waiting was inevitably under way.

As the morning light officially opened up a new September day, Wellum wandered around dispersal full of apprehension. Two of his friends were playing chess and Brian Kingcome was reading a book. Waiting to be scrambled was unanimously hated among the men. The sound of the telephone ringing caused everyone to jump, and in a matter of seconds Wellum's heart was racing as he hurried across the grass with eleven other pilots, all eager to get to their Spitfires.

Minutes later the Squadron were being vectored towards 150-plus bandits at Angels 12.

Flying as Kingcome's No. 2, Wellum closely followed him in a steady climb. The frightening anticipation of combat set in until Kingcome's call of 'Tally-ho!' sounded across the R/T. Easing off from his leader, Wellum stared

in awe at the incredible amount of aircraft in the sky. Keeping Kingcome in view, Wellum pressed the emergency boost override to increase his aircraft's speed and then began to seek out a target. The chaos of combat erupted. Gaggles of 109s dashed in all directions with malice in their wings.

Constantly checking his surroundings, Wellum set after a formation of Heinkel 111s splitting up in the tumult. He was abruptly interrupted, as tracers from behind forced him to dive down. The culprit was a 109. Wellum watched as the German climbed away with impressive speed. Turning the Spitfire in a wide circle, he caught sight of a lone Heinkel flying below towards the coast. Wellum dived down and settled into a good firing position. While taking return fire from the rear gunner, Wellum sprayed the He 111's fuselage and port engine, causing black smoke to stream out. The rear gunner put three holes in the Spitfire's port wing before Wellum silenced him with another squirt. The Heinkel began to slow down, and black smoke poured more thickly by the second. He fired the remainder of his ammunition into the wounded foe, and it gradually began to lose height. Wellum broke off and set course for Biggin.

....

Combat Report 11.9.40

Having lost the Squadron I was flying near the coast at 9,000 ft when I saw and engaged a He111. The port engine was out of action. I did a quarter attack and was met with fire from the top and bottom guns on the E/A. I did a second quarter attack and this time met only with fire from the top gun only. Black smoke began to come from his starboard engine. I did one more quarter attack and then went to astern. White smoke came from the starboard engine and the enemy aircraft lost height slowly. Having finished off my ammunition I broke off my engagement.

....

On Friday, 27 September, at 1500 hours, Wellum was airborne, patrolling with the Squadron at 15,000 feet when they spotted between fifteen and twenty Ju 88s that were being escorted by a large number of Bf 109s. The Squadron went for the bombers, attacking from head-on, beam, and from below, with the intention of scattering the formation. Wellum made sure he was in a decent position to make his attack. Flying below the bombers, Wellum picked out a Ju 88 and gave it a long and accurate burst of ammunition. Finding himself in a dangerous position with hordes of 109s looming above the scene, Wellum broke off, reminding himself of the number one rule: never fly straight and level for more than 20 seconds. Pulling out of an accelerated dive, Wellum levelled his Spitfire out and then sighted a Ju 88 that was breaking away from its formation. It appeared that three other Spitfires had also noticed the straying game and they too went after it guns blazing. Wellum followed suit and gave the 88 a short burst from long

Finding himself in a dangerous position with hordes of 109s looming above the scene, Wellum broke off, reminding himself of the number one rule: never fly straight and level for more than 20 seconds.

range as it dived towards the ground. The aircraft was finished, but the German crew were able to bale out. The empty machine finally crashed several miles south of Rochester. On his return back to base Wellum felt shattered and just wanted to get back on the ground. He was soaked in perspiration and felt slightly nauseous, so he slid back the Spitfire's hood, allowing the cool air to wash over him. Wellum would learn that the Squadron had fared well on this occasion, but at a cost. By 1550 hours only nine of the eleven aircraft scrambled had returned to base. After a while another Spitfire sounded across the aerodrome at Biggin Hill. It was Hugh Bowen-Morris, and his aircraft was in a spot of trouble. He crash-landed his Spitfire but fortuitously escaped unscathed. Now the only missing pilot was Sergeant Trevor Oldfield, but sadly he would not return. The Squadron later learned that Oldfield had crashed in Spitfire R6622 in Hesketh Park at around 1518 hours, after presumably being bounced by a 109. Ground witnesses suggested that the young pilot had bravely remained with his doomed aircraft to avoid crashing into the densely populated area surrounding the park.

Throughout the Battle of Britain Geoff Wellum continued to overcome his fears of mortal combat on a daily basis as he valiantly flew side by side with his fellow pilots in a squadron of which he was enormously proud to be a part. ■

After an engagement with the Luftwaffe over Eastbourne at 1615 hours on 17 November 1940, Wellum recorded the following report detailing his combat experience.

Combat Report 17.11.40

I was flying as Red 2 in the Squadron when we saw and attacked some 109's. I observed one 109 in a shallow dive and going very fast out to sea; he was leaving a smoke trail.

I chased him astern and fired a long burst at the enemy aircraft and saw tracer going into him. At once the enemy aircraft's dive steepened. I fired another good burst which resulted in the smoke trail thickening a lot which I think was due to glycol. The enemy aircraft's dive steepened still further to about 70 and I last saw the 109 going into cloud, and it seemed that it started to turn slowly on to its back, but this cannot be certain.

I attacked another enemy aircraft and fired one short burst which I observed to go into the enemy. This aircraft which was diving at the time continued its dive out to sea.

Wing Commander
Tom Neil, DFC*, AFC, Bronze Star (USA)

PILOT OFFICER TOM NEIL.

OUR DAY IN A FIGHTER SQUADRON STARTED ONE hour before dawn and went on to one hour after dusk. This meant that we were on duty from about 3.30 am during the summer and autumn of 1940 and stood down at about 10.30 in the evening. That is of course, when we were not called upon to fly throughout the night, which occasionally happened.

On the morning of 15 September 1940, Tom Neil was shaken from his sleep and scrambled with his fellow pilots of No. 249 Squadron. Leaving the grass airfield at North Weald, the Hurricanes lifted off and began to climb away from the aerodrome.

With tired eyes, the pilots rigorously scanned the arena for the opposing Hun. Flying as Yellow 2, Neil watched

With the gun button set to fire, Neil closed in and sprayed the port side of the Do 17.

as Bf 109s flew over several thousand feet above. Soon after, ack-ack began to thump into the air at the approaching formation of Dornier 17 bombers. The Squadron turned towards them to attack. Neil positioned himself slightly below and dead astern to the nearest aircraft. With the gun button set to fire, Neil closed in and sprayed the port side of the Do 17. After putting in a second burst, Neil fell back to maintain his position and watched in amazement as two large objects were flung from the Do 17. In a flash, Neil looked up as two men passed over his Hurricane with undeveloped parachutes. The crew had baled out and almost collided with their startled attacker. Suddenly, Neil was in the presence of hungry 109s looking for trouble. After some intense manœuvring and fighting, Neil looked around to find he was alone. The action had disappeared as quickly as it had started.

Neil kept his head turning in all directions, knowing full well that there could be hidden bandits skulking in the vast amounts of cumulus cloud. Sure enough, he spotted a Dornier slightly above him. Neil opened up the throttle and set after it. Flying high above the Thames, he quickly caught up with the Do 17, realising that he was not alone. About 200 yards on Neil's left was a Spitfire, chasing after the bomber in front. Hurricane and Spitfire flew line abreast and watched as the Hun took cover in the large cotton-wool clouds. It quickly re-emerged and

took evasive action, diving towards the Estuary. Neil and his companion began astern attacks, taking it in turns to fire short bursts into the Dornier. With smoking engines, the aircraft turned eastwards towards the sea. After a final attack, the Hurricane's guns fell silent. Neil watched the Spitfire deliver the remainder of its ammunition and then pull away. Exhausted, the stricken aircraft lost height and grazed over the convoy of ships below. Then the Dornier's tail slumped and collided with the North Sea. Leaving the aircraft to submerge in the waves, the RAF's finest veered away.

The two British pilots flew inland together, until the Spitfire pilot gave a wave from the cockpit and pulled away, leaving Neil to head back for North Weald. The Spitfire pilot who assisted Neil in this action was Pilot Officer Eric Lock of No. 41 Squadron. In Lock's combat report he included that he had witnessed Neil destroy an additional two 109s during this engagement. ∎

The following combat report was made by Tom Neil after flying as Yellow 2 with No. 249 Squadron on an afternoon sortie.

....

`Combat Report 27/9/40`

```
The squadron attacked formation of 10+
Junkers 88. After giving one burst full
deflection, the result of which was not
observed, I attacked a Ju 88 form astern
& gave a 4 sec burst. The starboard engine
burst into flames & large pieces fell off
the E A which turned over & went down
pouring smoke & glycol. Later with P/O
Millington I attacked another Junkers 88.
I fired all my ammunition & E A came down
from 18000 & crashed in the sea, 1 mile
off Shoreham. Both occupants were seen
in water together with boat but all
subsequently sank.
```
....

Wing Commander
Terence Kane

P/O TERENCE M. KANE
234 SQN.

On Sunday, 22 September 1940, air activity was drastically reduced because of the dull, foggy weather over the south of England. The morning was overcast, but began to clear throughout the afternoon, which encouraged a small number of Luftwaffe raiders into the air. However, the only enemy encountered was a lone Junkers Ju 88, which was attacked by two Spitfires of No. 234 Squadron. Flying as Red 1, Sergeant Alan Harker sighted the enemy aircraft heading in a westerly direction at 24,000 feet and gave chase, climbing into the sun with Flying Officer Terence Kane in tow. The Bolton-born sergeant pilot had already established himself as an efficient marksman in the air, for he had claimed several enemy aircraft as damaged and destroyed. Flying Officer Kane had only recently joined the Squadron and discovered he was piloting an aircraft

unrecognisable sky. Kane recalls what happened next:

Suddenly I came across two Me 109s. They did not immediately see me and I lined up behind the nearest one, closed into about 100 yards and fired on him. It burst into flames and fell into the clouds, but the second one had manœuvred into a position to attack me and the next thing I knew there was a small explosion in my engine, which promptly stopped. At once I dived into the clouds to evade the Me 109.

With no engine, Kane was forced to abandon his aircraft. At such a nerve-racking time, he tried to remain as calm as possible. Kane slid the hood back, unfastened his Sutton harness and then turned the Spitfire onto its back and began to climb out. Realising that he was still

...Kane turned the aircraft over and finally fell clear into open space. After some desperately worrying moments trying to find the ripcord, he pulled it and opened his chute just in the nick of time.

that was not as fast as Red 1's proved to be. Harker caught up with the Junkers about 50 miles south-east of Start Point. Despite its evasive tactics, Harker delivered an accurate attack from 150–100 yards, which caused pieces of metal to fly off the bomber as it began to lose height, emitting smoke. Satisfied with his attack, Harker broke off and turned for home. With plenty of petrol still in the tank, Kane raced after the Ju 88 to confirm its end.

Combat Report 22nd Sept 1940

```
I was Red 2 and took off at 16.35. We
spotted enemy at 24,000 feet, 5 miles SW
of base. Pursued and after Red 1 had
attacked I followed making a beam attack.
Starboard engine was on fire and a/c was
losing height rapidly when I continued
attack. Finally crashed into sea.
```

The following day Flying Officer Kane found himself in a dangerous predicament high above the clouds. After flying into the sun with another Spitfire, Kane was unable to keep up with the aircraft in front and soon became separated from his section. Owing to a faulty R/T, Kane was unable to communicate with anyone in the air or on the ground and was left alone in a vast,

connected to the R/T and oxygen tank, he climbed back into the cockpit to detach himself. Again, Kane turned the aircraft over and finally fell clear into open space. After some desperately worrying moments trying to find the ripcord, he pulled it and opened his chute just in the nick of time. After falling from about 400 or 500 feet, Kane landed in the cold sea and was soon picked up by a German ship, which fished him out of the Channel. Once he was on board, the Germans remarked: 'For you the war is over.'

Although a prisoner of war, the London-born flying officer was extremely lucky to be alive. Kane estimates that, if he had pulled the ripcord a few seconds later than he did, then he would not have survived the fall.

Terence Michael Kane spent just over four and a half years in a POW camp, finishing up in Stalag Luft III. ■

Wing Commander
Bob Foster, DFC

AS THE WAR DRUMS BEGAN TO SOUND THROUGH-out Europe, many young men began to think seriously about their possible options, and Bob Foster was no exception. He was absolutely certain that he did not want to be a soldier and fight in the trenches; instead he would enlist in the Royal Air Force Volunteer Reserve, because somehow air combat seemed far more glorious to the 18-year-old boy from south London.

Serving with No. 605 Squadron in September 1940, Foster caught his first glimpse of war when the Squadron arrived at its new post in Croydon. At about six o'clock in the evening, when Foster was bringing his Hurricane into land, he saw London burning. It was an unsettling introduction to Foster's new station. The severity of war had finally hit home, and soon enough Foster would be a part of it.

Not long after his arrival, the Squadron was in action. Soaring high above Sussex, a crowd of Messerschmitt 110s had formed up in a tight defensive circle, having lost the bombers they were supposed to be escorting. Foster and the boys of No. 605 Squadron dived into attack, intent on stopping the invaders' homeward dash across the Channel. The Hurricanes sped into the mix, passing black crosses and tracer bullets. Foster pressed his thumb into the gun button and awoke the blazing guns,

At about six o'clock in the evening, when Foster was bringing his Hurricane into land, he saw London burning.

when suddenly he heard an almighty explosion as his own engine blew up. Foster's instinctive reaction was to get out, but he decided against it. Glycol was streaming from the aircraft, so Foster turned the fuel off and increased his oxygen; luckily nothing was burning. Foster began to search the ground for somewhere to land. Soon enough the nervous pilot spotted a large field below. Foster began to make necessary checks before taking the Hurricane down.

I could get my wheels down (flaps wouldn't come down, but my wheels came down), so I thought ok, we will go in. I did quite a good dead-stick landing, which was quite nice, but it was a big field. It turned out to be Gatwick Airport. Not the Gatwick we know now, but it was still a big field. As I was coming into land, a 110 came crashing down right in front of the control tower, blew up. I got out of my aeroplane and it

hadn't burned, so a chap came up and said 'Are you alright?' I said, 'Yes thank you.' He said, 'Did you shoot that down?' I said, 'I don't know, maybe, perhaps I did.' He said, 'I just wondered, it all blew up and I have this chap's ear here if you would like it?' I didn't take his ear, but that was the sort of feeling; this chap thought he was doing me a good turn.

Foster would continue to fight for the sky in the coming weeks and months ahead, ever mindful of the lessons he was being taught.

You didn't hang around. You went into the bombers or what-ever it was, you hit hard, you got out again. You didn't stay around to see how good you were or if you had hit… because that would really ask for trouble. ∎

The following is a combat report made by Bob Foster after he had returned from a patrol with his squadron.

Combat Report 26.10/40

Whilst patrolling in pairs with 605 Squadron at 27,000 ft. We sighted 12-16 Me. 109's flying N.W. at approximately the same height. We attacked from the port quarter developing into a stern attack. The majority of the enemy commenced to climb a few however dived down. I followed one of them down closing gradually. At about 17,000 ft. he straightened out. I gave him a burst and noticed my ammunition hitting him. He immediately commenced to dive again and I followed him down giving him several short bursts. When at 11,000 ft. I closed rapidly to 75 yds. and gave him a 5 sec. burst. Pieces fell off the machine and he turned over on his back and dived almost vertically through the clouds. I followed him through but lost him. The position was approximately between Woodchurch and Tenterden.

Squadron Leader
Tony Iveson, DFC

SQN/LDR TONY IVESON
616 'F' SQN BATTLE OF BRITAIN
617 'DAMBUSTER' SQN

DAVID PRITCHARD

On the morning of 16 September 1940, Sergeant Tony Iveson found that he was alone at 15,000 feet in his damaged Spitfire. He was flying over the North Sea and positioned a long way out, east of the English coast. Tony retells the story:

The rear gunner of a German bomber had opened up with accurate return fire just as I lined up the sights of my eight Browning machine guns. There were a few thumps as bullets hit the engine and took a piece off the corner of the windshield. As my aircraft fell away, the Junkers disappeared, and when I recovered control and looked around, the sky was empty. Where now? Obviously, turn west and try for my airfield.

The engine was running roughly, so I eased back the throttle. A quick check on temperature and pressure — not good. One slightly above normal, the other below. The question was forming in my mind, and I didn't like it. 'Would it get me back to Kirton Lindsey in north Lincolnshire?'

After three hours at readiness that morning, three Spitfires of No. 616 (South Yorkshire) Auxiliary Squadron were scrambled to give air cover to a naval convoy off the east coast.

Flying circles round and round the collection of ships seemed routine until the sky above sprouted black shell bursts and through them we spotted another aircraft at a much higher level. 'Tally Ho!' I heard through my earphones, as Flight Lieutenant Colin MacFie and Pilot Officer Phil Leckrone (an American) opened up and climbed away streaming black smoke. I followed but soon found I was losing them, even though I pushed the throttle through the gate of my not very sprightly Spitfire. New sergeant pilots were usually given the oldest machines on the Squadron! Also, I hadn't a lot of experience, having flown only 10 hours on type before joining 616. Engine handling then was a mystery, as was maximum boost override and fuel consumption at different throttle settings!

Trying to keep my eyes on the dots ahead of me in the long climb after the fast enemy aircraft which turned out to be a Junkers 88, I saw my two companions engage without any obvious effect and then turn away. I never saw them again. Slowly I got closer and closer to the violently weaving Junkers, and then the gunner suddenly opened up and I was in trouble!

After settling down a bit, trying to hold on to altitude and nurse the engine at the same time, I was aware the altimeter was slowly unwinding and the radiator temperature slowly increasing. Sky and ocean were empty, as I anxiously worked out the best course to steer, remembering that Norfolk jutted out further eastwards than Lincolnshire. Steadily, my ailing Spitfire eased lower and lower until suddenly, on the far horizon of the sun-illuminated grey sea, a number of dots. What was it? Closer and closer I steered. At last I identified a convoy. Hope returned to my heart! Whether it was the one we had circled I knew not. Nor did I care. I headed straight for them.

When I realised I might not reach them, I prepared for the inevitable ducking. I undid my parachute straps and tightened my harness; took off my helmet and stuffed it behind the seat. Pushed back and locked the hood open, then put down the small side door. I remembered one instruction — land along the waves and not into them. The engine was making unhappy noises and running very roughly, but I still had speed and control. No wheels or flaps down. Try to put the tail in first and hold off as long as possible to get the landing speed down. Splash and a bounce! I pulled the quick release, my straps fell away and with the second touchdown I was thrown face first against the windshield! At this second splash I was out of the cockpit pronto and on to the wing. The Spitfire nosed down and disappeared past me beneath the waves, leaving me floating in my Mae West lifejacket watching a lifeboat being launched from the nearest ship. Forty-five minutes later strong hands hauled a sodden and shivering sergeant pilot into their boat. 'You're all right now, mate!' they said.

On board HMS Staunch, a trawler cum minesweeper, in the hot engine room, wrapped in some sailor's dungarees and being filled up with steaming cocoa lavishly laced with rum, I stopped shaking and began to feel I had survived.

The following morning an RAF rescue launch arrived alongside and took me off in my salt-stiff uniform. We landed at Lowestoft to find transport waiting to take me to RAF Coltishall, near Norwich. 'Right,' said the Flight Sergeant 'You are just the bloke we're looking for. We've got a Spitfire for 616 Squadron, you can deliver it.' What else to say? 'Right, Flight!'

No helmet, no parachute, just an uncomfortable leather cushion. Climb in, do up the straps, quick cockpit check, start up, all OK, chocks away, taxi on to the field, get a green from the control tower, open up, deafened by the engine noise, take off, head north, clear day, find the Wash, then Lincoln — a great landmark the Cathedral — find the straight road past RAF Scampton, find Kirton Lindsey. Land, taxi in, 'This is for you Flight Sergeant, from Coltishall.' Not much fuss about my return. 'Better see the MO with that face of yours.' Good chap, that doc. 'What have you been up to? Any feeling of shock?' 'Not particularly,' I answered. 'Good show, take a few days leave, here's a chit for the adjutant.' I did as I was told! I was 21 years and 6 days old. ■

Group Captain
Herbert Moreton Pinfold

SQN/LDR
HERBERT MORETON PINFOLD
OC. 56 SQN BATTLE OF BRITAIN

DAVI·PRITCHARD

HERBERT PINFOLD WAS BORN ON 5 FEBRUARY 1913 and he joined the RAF on a short service commission in September 1934. Early beginnings in the RAF took him to Ismailia, Egypt, with No. 6 Squadron and to Martlesham Heath with No. 64 Squadron. After serving at different stations with varying roles such as a Flying Instructor and Adjutant, Pinfold was sent to Ashton Down for a refresher course. After five hours' conversion to Hurricanes at No. 5 OTU, Squadron Leader

"…at about 16,000' while flying due south I saw the enemy formation of God knows how many Do. 215's and Me's 110 above…"

Pinfold took command of No. 56 Squadron on 24 August 1940. By this time, the Squadron was stationed at North Weald, where they were having great difficulties. The Squadron had lost both its flight commanders after they had been shot down shortly before Pinfold's arrival.

Within the next five days, Pinfold flew fourteen operational sorties, three in one day with only seven pilots available. During those tense flights, Pinfold shot at several German bomber aircraft, but was unable to make specific claims.

On 1 September the Squadron was sent to Boscombe Down. Pinfold recalled:

Fighter Command HQ decided that, to enable No. 56 Squadron to rebuild with new pilots including Polish and Czechoslovakian, and still remain operational, it should exchange bases with 249 Squadron at Boscombe Down, but for technical reasons 56 Squadron aircraft and ground crew were to remain at North Weald. This led to much confusion with postings and records.

On 30 September No. 56 Squadron intercepted a large formation of bombers escorted by fighters heading for the aircraft factory at Yeovil. On this encounter, Squadron Leader Pinfold shot down a Do 215 and was hit in the glycol tank by return fire. As a result, fumes filled his cockpit and his engine overheated, but Pinfold was fortunate enough to make a forced landing at Warmwell.

One particular fond memory for Moreton Pinfold is of an incident that took place at North Weald during the Battle of Britain. He was in a fierce battle of squash with his good friend Victor Beamish and out of nowhere a raid came over. 'We had better get going!' Pinfold remarked. 'Sod off, we'll finish this game, I'm winning!' Beamish replied. Hence the battle continued on both fronts. ■

Combat Report 30.9.40

```
Portland Bill at 22,000 ft. I climbed the
Squadron slightly to the West of Portland
Bill to gain the advantage of the sun, and
at about 16,000' while flying due South
I saw the enemy formation of God knows how
many Do. 215's and Me's 110 above, the
bombers being at 19,000' and the fighters
5,000' above and behind. The Do's were in
vics of three line astern and the Me's 110
were circling. All the Do's suddenly opened
fire at the same time. I climbed the
Squadron up to about 19,000' and slowly
turned in towards the enemy formation to
deliver our attack from the rear quarter.
I closed to about 400 yds. with the enemy
fighters coming down on us and I do not
think they had seen us. I then opened fire
at a Do.215 from rear quarter giving a
five second burst closing to about 125
yrds. While I was closing the E/A opened
fire and one shot must have hit my A/C
as Glycol fumes immediately filled the
cockpit. I broke away and force landed at
Warmwell. P/O. Higginson saw the Do I had
attacked going downwards with both engines
pouring black smoke.
```

Flight Lieutenant
Charles 'Tich' Palliser, DFC, AE

SERGEANT/PILOT
CHARLES "TICH" PALLISER

DAVID PRITCHARD

Charles (TICH) Palliser
43 & 249 Sqd

CHARLES PALLISER WAS BORN IN WEST HARTLEPOOL on 11 January 1919. In June 1939 he joined the RAFVR and was called up to full-time service at the outbreak of war. In July 1940 Palliser converted to Hurricanes at Sutton Bridge and was posted to No. 17 Squadron at Debden. On 14 September he joined No. 249 Squadron at North Weald.

The following day was Sunday, 15 September 1940, the most climactic day of the Battle of Britain. It was on this day that the Luftwaffe sustained tremendous losses to its bomber forces and that Britain finally triumphed over Hitler's orders for the Luftwaffe to gain air supremacy over the RAF.

On this memorable day, Charles Palliser was found patrolling the skies in a Hurricane with his Squadron. During the late-afternoon patrol, Palliser became separated from A Flight over south-west London. After cruising around at 14,000 feet, he noticed a Dornier Do 17 travelling in a northerly direction, flying in and out of cloud at 9,000 feet. Palliser dived and made a steep quarter attack, opening fire at approximately 350 yards. The 3-second burst scored direct hits between the starboard engine and cockpit. Palliser then noticed a Spitfire was attacking the same aircraft and spotted thick black smoke pouring from the Do 17's port engine. Before Palliser broke off from the attack, he observed four Germans evacuating their aircraft by parachute. On his return, Palliser claimed the Dornier as a 'half one destroyed'.

On 26 September, Palliser once again damaged a Dornier Do 17 near Gravesend on an afternoon patrol.

The following morning, flying near Redhill with Red

The stricken aircraft went into a steep turn with smoke and oil pouring from the starboard engine...

Section, Palliser engaged a large circle of Messerschmitt 110s. As Red 3, Palliser dived on the formation from 19,000 feet, which divided the 110s. In the chaos, Palliser became separated from his section but managed to attack a 110, giving it two lethal bursts. Palliser's ammunition sprayed the 110's cabin, fuselage and engine, silencing the top gunner. The stricken aircraft went into a steep turn with smoke and oil pouring from the starboard engine, before ending up on the pier, several

miles from the coast south of Redhill.

Palliser then attacked a second 110, causing its port engine to cough smoke. It went into a gradual dive, but Palliser was unable to witness its fate.

As if this exhausting brawl was not enough, Palliser then engaged with a third 110, but he had to break off when a rear gunner put a cannon shell through his rudder. By this time, Palliser's ammunition boxes were empty.

Combat Report 26/9/40

```
I was Red Three in section flying above
9/10 cloud, height 14,000 ft. on being
vectored to Gravesend. Following Red Leader
I saw E/A about 3-4 miles ahead travelling
South. I dived following Red Leader and
made a beam attack developing into a
quarter attack giving two bursts of 4
secs. As I attacked I could see white
smoke coming from starboard engine. There
was no return fire. As I broke away E/A
dived into cloud.
```

At 16,000 feet over the Thames Estuary on 7 November 1940, Palliser was flying as Blue 2 on an afternoon sortie when he noticed bombs bursting around a convoy below. Being in the rear section of the Squadron, Palliser circled down slowly when, at about 5,000 feet, he spotted a Bf 109 diving below his position. Palliser followed him and held his fire until the 109 pulled out of its dive. He carried out an attack from above at close range, raking the enemy aircraft from nose to tail with one long burst of about 7 seconds. The 109 spun away out of control and crashed in the mouth of the Estuary, about 5 miles north-east of Margate. Palliser returned to North Weald, claiming a Messerschmitt 109 as destroyed. The claim was also confirmed by Red 2. ∎

Flight Lieutenant
Peter Hairs, MBE

ON 12 MAY 1940, PILOT OFFICER PETER HAIRS joined No. 501 Squadron in France. The tragic crash of the Bristol Bombay transport aircraft had happened the day before, so things were tense around the camp.

The Bombay accident had claimed the lives of three Squadron members and the Bombay crew, as well as injuring six others, including Byron Duckenfield. In his own words, Duckenfield remembered:

Arriving over the destination airfield at Betheniville (near Epernay), the Bombay pilot approached to land but aborted the landing, being too high on final approach at the airfield boundary. Going round again, the pilot made a second attempt but it was apparent to me, looking out of a fuselage window, that the aircraft was still much too high at about 200 feet above the airfield.

What happened next he learned afterwards from eye-witness friends on the ground.

The aircraft was – at about 200' – too high on final approach. When the engines were throttled back, the nose of the aircraft rose quickly to near-vertical; the aircraft stalled and began a tail-slide, falling rapidly backward. Just before

With shrapnel lodged in his back, Hairs landed his Hurricane in a field and was met by a French soldier and his rifle.

impact with the ground, the fuselage levelled and the aircraft hit the ground flat. The fact that the aircraft had levelled just before impact saved most of those on board from fatal injury, but still there were five fatalities.

Soon after his arrival, on 15 May, Pilot Officer Hairs was involved in his first action, flying as No. 2 to his Flight Commander. They sighted and attacked a formation of Dornier 17 bombers.

While trying to keep one of the bombers in his sights, Hairs was concentrating so intently that he had forgotten he had been flying in formation, until he noticed his Flight Commander's Hurricane close to his own – in his own words 'Too close!'

Despite the worrying predicament they were in, the Dornier was shot down and confirmed, with Hairs

claiming a share.

In early June 1940 Hairs continued to fly sweeps over France with the Squadron. On one occasion, when he was climbing in line astern with his section, an explosion occurred somewhere underneath his seat. Hairs had been bounced by a 109, which had dived down at his aircraft, firing cannon shells. With shrapnel lodged in his back, Hairs landed his Hurricane in a nearby field and was met by a French soldier and his rifle. A jeep soon arrived with two British army officers, and Hairs was taken back to their unit to recuperate. Hairs took the train to Paris and then caught up with his Squadron in Le Mans the following day.

On a morning patrol in September 1940, Hairs was flying as Yellow 1 over Maidstone when he spotted a section of Bf 109s flying at 20,000 feet. As the chase began, Hairs tailed a 109 that was trying to evade its pursuer by twisting and turning but ultimately to no avail. Hairs thumbed the gun button, firing a succession of bursts until his ammunition was used up. The 109 appeared to be in a bad way, as white smoke and glycol bled out into the summer air. ∎

Combat Report 18.9.40

```
I was leading the second section (Yellow)
of 501 Squadron, when we were ordered to
patrol Maidstone at 20,000 ft. After
orbiting for a few minutes I saw about
4 Me 109's on our right at about the same
altitude. One of these turned in front of
me. I therefore turned left onto his tail.
He immediately flew off in a South
Easterly direction, twisting about and
losing height. Eventually [in] range and
fired a number of bursts until my
ammunition was finished. White smoke and
glycol came from E/A, which was losing
height rapidly. I last saw E/A at about
500 ft and about 5 miles from French
coast, with black puffs of smoke coming
from it, so that it is unlikely that it
got home.
```

Squadron Leader
Robert 'Bob' Kings

F/O R.A. "Bob" Kings
238 SQN

David Pritchard

R.A. Kings

AFTER COMPLETING HIS TRAINING AND CONVERTING to Hurricanes at No. 6 Operational Training Unit at Sutton Bridge, Pilot Officer Bob Kings was posted to No. 238 Squadron at St Eval on 31 August 1940.

On 25 September Pilot Officer Kings was flying with B Flight as Blue 3 when the Squadron engaged an enemy raid consisting of He 111s and Bf 110s in the proximity of Bristol. Kings fired at an enemy aircraft at the rear of the formation, giving it a 4-second burst from about 200 yards. When Kings was astern to the straggler, he gave it another long burst of 6 seconds while closing in, despite the rear gunner doing his best to put him off. Violently breaking off to starboard, Kings saw big pieces fall away from the 111's starboard engine. Having fired 1,600 rounds, Kings pulled back on the control column and climbed to regain height. With no enemy in sight and being unable to contact the Squadron, Kings landed at Bath and then later returned to Middle Wallop.

The following day at 1625 hours Kings engaged mass formations of Bf 110s and He 111s with his Squadron over the Isle of Wight. Flying as Yellow 2 in A Flight, Kings climbed to somewhere between 14,000 and 16,000 feet before spotting an He 111 in his location. After lining the target up in his gunsight, Kings gave the bomber a series of short bursts, which scored direct hits. As flames began to lick from the 111's starboard engine, Kings' Hurricane was hit by a rear gunner (believed to be from a Bf 110). Kings broke away from the action, but his cockpit began to fill up with smoke and flames began emerging from the cockpit floor. With no other option but to evacuate his aircraft, Kings slid the hood back and baled out. Eventually, he landed safely near Newport and then returned to Middle Wallop.

Later, witnesses informed Kings that they had seen the enemy aircraft crash in flames. They had also seen his Hurricane crash close by to where he had landed.

```
Combat Report 26/09/40

I was yellow 2 and I attacked with
Squadron. I climbed and then saw E/A which
I identified as a HE 111 and carried out
quarter attack developing to astern firing
short 2 sec burst from quarter + continuing
with 2-3 sec bursts from astern at range
of 200-250 yds closing. The starboard
engine had flames coming out of it, and
lurched over to left + then righted
itself. I experienced fire from rear gun
```

```
and after breaking away there was smoke in
my cockpit and as soon as I slid cover
back flames increased considerably + whole
of bottom of cockpit was on fire. I baled
out and landed about 2-3 miles W of
Newport quite near my a/c. Some of the
army authorities informed me they had
witnessed the encounter and saw E/A crash
in flames. They also saw my Hurricane
crash. Returned to Middle Wallop.
```

Four days later, Kings was forced to bale out yet again after colliding with Pilot Officer V. C. Simmonds during a routine patrol. Both pilots survived the crash, but Kings was injured in a heavy landing because of a damaged

Violently breaking off to starboard, Kings saw big pieces fall away from the 111's starboard engine.

parachute. The wounded Pilot Officer was admitted to hospital. His Hurricane crashed near Shaftesbury.

For many years after the war a humorous and light-hearted banter existed between Kings and Simmonds about who was responsible for the collision. The verdict was mutually and privately agreed just before Simmonds passed away. ∎

Squadron Leader
Tony Pickering

SERGEANT/PILOT
TONY PICKERING 32 AND 501 SQDNS

David Pritchard

As a young Leicestershire village boy of 18 years in late 1938–early 1939, and as an ex-Grammar School boy serving an engineering apprenticeship with BTH, I realised that war was inevitable. I had seen aircraft and airships, but then an RAF biplane fighter landed owing to lack of fuel in a field near our house and the airship R101 flew overhead, and I thus was encouraged to fly as a pilot myself. In early 1939 I applied to join the RAFVR. I was flying solo on Tiger Moth aircraft before the war started on 3 September 1939. Being called up into the RAF on 1 September, I was trained as a fighter pilot.

Sergeant Pilot Tony Pickering was posted to No. 32 Squadron in July 1940, the first month of the Battle of Britain. Stationed at Biggin Hill, Pickering was given an introduction to the robust Hawker Hurricane, an aircraft he had not even seen before.

The Hurricane was a strongly built and designed aircraft and was capable of taking heavy damage, more so than the Spitfire or Me 109, but was inferior in speed to them, and was thus used predominately against bombers. I was given

"…when he was at about 500 feet diving towards the ground I gave him my last bursts…"

one practice flight in a Hurricane and I was sent on operational flights the next morning at Hawkinge forward base airfield. The Squadron Commander realised that myself and two other young inexperienced pilots would not survive, and sent us on the following day to a training unit at Sutton Bridge.

On their return to Biggin Hill in mid-August, No. 32 Squadron was sent to Gravesend for a rest and re-formation, and the new recruits were sent to No. 501 Squadron. Speaking of his time with 501, Tony recalls:

The Squadron had been through the evacuation from France and had some experienced pilots. We junior pilots were assisted by the experienced sergeant pilots and officer pilots, but there was no time for combat training. We flew head-on attacks on the German bombers, bombing airfields and London docks, flying through the large formations, firing our guns before being chased away by the Me 109 fighters.

In September, Pickering survived being shot down in flames by Bf 109s after confronting 300 German bombers. He baled out of his aircraft unhurt and returned to active duty.

On 29 October, Pickering got his retribution when he claimed a Bf 109 destroyed. An extract from Tony's combat report adds further details:

```
I closed in to 300 yards and saw it [Bf
109] was yellow with large black crosses
on the upper surface of the wings. I
immediately opened fire from dead astern
and he went into a dive turning and
twisting to evade my fire. I followed him
down firing short bursts all the time and
when he was at about 500 feet diving
towards the ground I gave him my last
bursts which set fire to his starboard
petrol tank and he immediately blew up.
The pilot did not bale out. The aircraft
crashed at Ham Street approximately 15
miles north-west of Dungeness.
```

In conclusion, Tony recalls that, thanks to the 'ground crews, Army personnel, WAAF and Observation Corps, the Navy and also RAF Bomber Command, the Hun did not gain control of the sky'. ∎

Squadron Leader
Cyril 'Bam' Bamberger, DFC*

Sgt/Pilot Cyril "Bam" Bamberger
41 Sqdn

Dav Pritchard

Sergeant Pilot Cyril Bamberger's first day in combat left him feeling lost and a little bit unsure of things. On 21 August 1940 Bamberger was scrambled from Biggin Hill with No. 610 Squadron in the early hours of the morning with instructions to intercept a raid off the coast. As the Spitfires climbed to their given patrol line, the Squadron became separated in the cloudy sky and was unable successfully to engage the enemy. Bamberger felt bewildered by the experience. In one instant the sky seemed full of aircraft and in the next it was completely empty. How anyone was supposed to shoot down the enemy when the environment changed in a matter of seconds was anyone's guess. Bamberger was not alone in his confusion. However, as the Luftwaffe's attacks heightened, there would be plenty of opportunities to become accustomed to the bedlam of air warfare.

In mid-September, Bamberger reported to Hornchurch to join No. 41 Squadron. On the day he arrived the Squadron had four Spitfires shot down, and the following day Bamberger received word that his good friend Doug Corfe was injured in hospital, after having been shot down by the enemy. The latter end of September would at least bring some reprisal for the Sergeant Pilot.

The morning of 23 September brought fine weather over the south of England. Comprising part of No. 41 Squadron's A Flight, Bamberger found himself scrutinising the vast sky in search of enemy aircraft. At around 1015 the wait was over when 12 Bf 109s were seen at 25,000 feet. As No. 3 in Yellow Section, Bamberger sighted two 109s to starboard and below his position. He delivered a quarter attack on the nearest aircraft, which started to lose height, making no effort to evade his guns, but Bamberger peeled off from the pursuit to avoid falling victim to another 109's cannons.

Four days later Bamberger would again be mixing it up with a Messerschmitt 109. When flying as Yellow 3,

Bamberger veered after the escaping 109 and opened fire from below and astern. After a 3-second burst, Bamberger watched the enemy lose height, with smoke issuing from its engine or cockpit, but he was forced to break off from the attack because of a formation of enemy fighters preparing to dive from above. Bamberger managed to escape back to base after giving a Luftwaffe pilot something to think about on his way back to the French coast.

After being vectored towards the Kent coast on the morning of 5 October, the pilots of No. 41 Squadron perused the sky for the Hun and swept through the clouds in their ever-faithful Spitfires. Flying over Dungeness, the Squadron engaged a formation of yellow-nosed Bf 109s at approximately 26,000 feet. Bamberger was propelled into action.

Catching a 109 in his sights, Bamberger opened fire from a range of 150 yards and closing. The quick burst was enough to knock the aircraft, belonging to Alfred Zweis of JG 53, out of the sky. But rather than feeling elated with his success, Bamberger returned to Hornchurch feeling exhausted as usual. On this encounter, he had fired 800 rounds at the enemy. ■

....

Combat Report 5.10.40

```
I was Yellow 3 in a Squadron formation of
line astern. 3 Me.109's passed at right
angles to our course, below us. I broke
formation in a diving turn to the left and
came up astern of the port aircraft of the
enemy formation. I fired a burst from close
range and smoke and flames appeared about
the cockpit and engine of the 109. I then
broke off attack.
```

....

Bamberger veered after the escaping 109 and opened fire from below and astern.

Bamberger lost contact with the Squadron after being scattered by an attack fronted by 109s. In a solitary position, the Sergeant Pilot sighted a lone enemy fighter making his way back across the Channel from Dover.

Wing Commander
Peter Olver, DFC

THE **BATTLE OF BRITAIN IS GENERALLY STATED TO** have officially ended on 31 October 1940, because Britain was finally free from the threat of invasion. However, this did not mean that the intensity of aerial warfare over the Channel and the south of England ceased. In fact, this was far from the case.

Pilot Officer Peter Olver of No. 603 Squadron had already been awakened to the vicious realities of operations when, on 24 October, his Spitfire had been shot down by 109s over Hastings, forcing the green fighter pilot to bale out on his very first engagement with the enemy. To this day Olver believes that being shot down on that occasion was a positive experience, because it taught him a valuable lesson about aerial combat. From then on, Olver would be prepared.

On 11 November 1940 seven Spitfires of No. 603 Squadron were given the responsibility of protecting a convoy patrol over the Thames Estuary. While several other squadrons joined the sortie with varying roles to play, the 603 boys circled high above the convoy with No. 64 Squadron to counteract the enemy fighters, while others concentrated on the bombers. Soon enough the sky was full of smoke trails and twisting aircraft.

Flying as Blue 4, Pilot Officer Olver managed with relative ease to set his guns upon a Ju 87. He delivered a stern attack, firing a continual burst from 300 yards' range closing to just 15 yards, which caused the Stuka to fall in a shallow dive, with thick black smoke pouring from it. Olver passed over the top of the falling Ju 87 and then turned his Spitfire sharply to the right to outturn a Messerschmitt 109 that was making an attack. Olver latched onto the 109's tail and spent the remainder of his ammunition in three short bursts. With his first lesson of aerial combat in mind, Olver did not hang about to watch the 109's future. Instead he weaved around the sky with attentive eyes and set course for Hornchurch.

Combat Report 11/11/40

I was Blue 4. When on patrol with 603 Squadron I delivered a stern attack on a Ju.87 (the nearer of a Group) firing a continual burst from 300 yds. range closing to 15 yds. (approximately 1,800 rounds). I passed over the top of the Ju.87 and turned simultaneously sharply to the right and was immediately attacked by an Me.109. I got onto his tail and fired the remainder of my ammunition in 3 short

bursts at 150 - 200 yds. Range. The Ju.87 went down in a shallow dive with intense black smoke pouring out.

Just before Christmas 1940, Olver left No. 603 Squadron and joined No. 66 Squadron at Biggin Hill. On 29 December he flew a morning patrol over Dover and Dungeness as Blue 2, flying with Flight Lieutenant Christie in a section of two. During the patrol they spotted a Do 17 flying a couple of miles out to sea at around 4,000 feet. Obviously alarmed at the sight of two Spitfires, the Do 17 jettisoned its bombs and broke off

> To this day Olver believes that being shot down on that occasion was a positive experience, because it taught him a valuable lesson about aerial combat.

towards the clouds. Christie was the first to attack the aircraft, giving it a quick squirt from 200 yards. He continued to circle the aircraft, giving it deflection shots from above and below. The rear gunner was put out of action. Olver also attacked the bomber, firing short bursts from 300 yards and closing to 50 yards in a steep climb. He observed tracer bullets entering the machine but soon lost track of it because of cloud cover. Despite Blue Section's efforts, the damaged Dornier made it back across the Channel, after being escorted by some 109s coming out to meet it. Christie was the first to make it back to base, touching down at 1030 with empty ammunition boxes, and Olver returned to the aerodrome 10 minutes later. ■

Squadron Leader
Jocelyn 'Joss' Millard

P/O JOCELYN GEORGE POWER MILLARD
1 AND 242 SQN

DAVIPRITCHARD

WHEN JOCELYN GEORGE POWER MILLARD announced his plans to fly in the RAF, his mother, like most at the time, had her reservations about her son's chosen career path. In the First World War, she had sadly lost her husband in the submarine service, so respecting her son's decision to join the air force was not something that came easily for her. Millard recalled: 'It drove my mother mad talking about flying aircraft, but I made up my mind that I was going. I joined the RAF in 1937. My mother got over it, she had to.'

Millard's remark perhaps seems insensitive out of context, but the truth of the matter is that he was deeply patriotic and he wanted to follow in his father's footsteps by serving his country. In 1937 he joined the RAFVR and began to pursue his desires to fly.

While Millard was busy completing the necessary training courses to become a fighter pilot, his school friend Basil Pyne was serving in France, with No. 73 Squadron. On one occasion, Basil advised Millard that if he ever got the opportunity to fly Hurricanes then he should do it!

Millard's chance arrived on 4 September 1940, when he was posted to No. 6 Operational Training Unit at Sutton Bridge. It was here that Millard converted to the Hawker Hurricane and the experience was utterly fulfilling: 'The Hurricane was a wonderful aircraft in every way. They were like a War Horse, you felt empowered. The Hurricane had a tighter turning circle than the 109, but the 109 was slightly faster. Generally speaking though, they were comparable.'

On 21 September Pilot Officer Millard was posted to No. 1 Squadron at Wittering. During a practice flight he flew south of his station to Baldock in Hertfordshire to entertain a certain young lady who was expecting him at

"We had no tomorrow, so there was no point in making plans..."

3.30 p.m. On Millard's arrival he decided to impress the onlookers by flying around a church steeple, but he flew so low and close to it that he almost knocked it off. Unfortunately for Millard, an irate bystander decided to jot down his aircraft markings and thereafter filed a complaint. To his utter displeasure, Millard was grounded for a week, and, for a young man wearing white wings on his chest, it was the worst kind of punishment. Not

long after Millard moved on to Douglas Bader's No. 242 Squadron stationed at Coltishall.

Throughout his time in a front-line fighter squadron, Millard's greatest fear was not being shot down by the enemy, nor was it being burned − a fear that haunted most fighter pilots − but rather a horrid fear of a mid-air collision. After all, tight formation flying in a sky full of twisting aircraft certainly made such a thing plausible. Fortunately for Millard, his fear would never come to fruition.

After serving with No. 242 Squadron, Millard would go on to join No. 615 Squadron at Northolt on 3 November.

A few months later Millard was posted to CFS, Upavon, in March 1941, for an instructor's course, and the following month he joined the staff at FTS, Cranwell. In September 1941 Millard began instructing in Canada at 35 SFTS.

Throughout his time in different fighter squadrons, flying patrols through dangerous skies, Millard found that his faith in God was a huge help and comfort to him. 'We had no tomorrow, so there was no point in making plans, because you just didn't know what was going to happen. I was fortunate. I said some prayers to keep me alive and they worked.' ■

Squadron Leader
Graham Leggett

Graham Percival Leggett's association with the Hawker Hurricane began when he was an apprentice at the Hawker factory at Kingston. It was at this factory that he worked on the first production Hurricane. To see his work in action, Leggett would cycle to the Royal Air Force station at Northolt to see No. 111 Squadron show off its new Hurricanes at the Empire Air Day.

In 1940 Leggett was accepted for pilot training and was posted to an Operational Training Unit, where he was instructed by experienced pilots who were being rested after having served in various fighter squadrons in France.

After completing his training, Leggett joined No. 245 Squadron at Aldergrove, but soon moved to No. 46 Squadron at North Weald, where he served during the Battle of Britain.

During one of Leggett's early scrambles with the Squadron he encountered a formation of Bf 109s armed with bombs at 'twelve o'clock high'. Climbing in tight

...Leggett readied himself for action, but was suddenly shaken as a voice sounded over the R/T to 'Break port!'

formation with twelve aircraft in vics of three, Leggett readied himself for action, but was suddenly shaken as a voice sounded over the R/T to 'Break port!' With 109s diving down at them from above and more fighters approaching from astern, the Squadron turned into the fighters approaching from the port side. After some hectic seconds trying to adjust his goggles and oxygen mask, Leggett noticed an aircraft was already going down in flames. The pandemonium was both disorientating and yet at the same time exhilarating as aircraft from both sides broke off in different directions trying to evade or attack. After the heated conflict appeared to have cooled down, Leggett heard an instruction from his flight commander to re-form with the rest of the Squadron, which he obligingly did, before flying back to base, where he landed safely.

Some time later, on 11 November, at around 1405 hours, No. 46 Squadron was involved in an attack by Italian aircraft of the Regia Aeronautica. On this occasion Pilot Officer Leggett, flying as Red 2, sighted a formation of Fiat BR 20 bombers and climbed towards them. As he neared the formation with his section, one broke off in a

dive, seemingly in a spot of bother. Leggett gave it a squirt of ammunition from approximately 200 yards, as did other Hurricanes from his Squadron. The attacks provoked one of the bomber's crew to evacuate the aircraft by parachute. Turning back towards the formation, Leggett then attacked another on the far right of the group. He gave the aircraft a few short bursts, and the return fire ceased, the bomber falling behind its group before eventually crashing in a nearby wood.

Combat Report 11.11.1940

On sighting enemy bombers I opened out and climbed up in pursuit. As I neared formation one bomber dived away apparently in trouble but gave him a short burst - case he may have been bluffing. One of the crew baled out, however, and I broke off the attack. By now four bombers were left in formation, and I attacked the one on extreme right. After second attack he lagged behind formation and fire from gunner had ceased. A third attack was delivered during which I ran out of ammunition. The aircraft eventually crashed in a wood near Woodbridge.

Later, in June 1941, Leggett was posted to No. 249 Squadron in Malta – where the fight for the control of this strategically important island was well under way.

On 17 July Leggett destroyed an Italian Mc 200. However, on 21 December he was shot down and forced to bale out of his aircraft with slight injuries.

After recovering from this unfortunate incident and after being rested from operations, Leggett was posted to No. 73 Squadron in North Africa, where he returned to the air flying Hurricanes. ∎

Air Commodore
Charles Widdows, DFC

STANLEY CHARLES WIDDOWS WAS BORN IN BERKSHIRE, on 4 October 1909. He joined the RAF in September 1926, as an aircraft apprentice, and then later graduated from RAF Cranwell. By the time war was declared in September 1939, Widdows had a wealth of flying experience under his belt. He had served in a number of different squadrons over the years and had become an accomplished test pilot. While at Martlesham Heath, Widdows conducted extensive performance tests on the first production Hurricane and the first production Spitfire. Needless to say, his experience was invaluable.

On 16 July 1940 Widdows took command of No. 29 Squadron at Digby. At this time the Squadron was equipped with Blenheims, but towards the end of September they were re-equipped with Bristol Beaufighters — a twin engine, long-range heavy fighter.

On 13 March 1941 Wing Commander Widdows and his Observer Sergeant Ryall flew a protective patrol over Waddington in a Bristol Beaufighter. Shortly after 0230 hours a 'blip' appeared on the aircraft's Airborne Inter-

Still, the Ju 88 proved elusive, until visual contact was made a second time. Widdows fired from approximately 100 yards at the 88's starboard engine, which burst into flames.

ception Radar, 3 miles south-west of their position at 11,000 feet. The 'blip' flashed continuously, but the bandit turned to starboard and they lost track of it. Following suit, Widdows turned to starboard, and a second 'blip' appeared on the radar but disappeared after a few minutes. The Beaufighter was then directed towards a raid flying south-east. When approaching Boston at about 0323 hours, Widdows was directed towards an enemy aircraft flying north at 6,000 feet. In a matter of minutes Widdows sighted a Ju 88 ahead of him and closed in to attack. Widdows opened fire from dead astern, giving one short burst, which could be seen entering the 88's fuselage. The Junkers went into a dive from which it did not recover. The badly wrecked aircraft and three bodies were later found at Smiths Farm, Dovedale, near Louth, Lincolnshire.

In the early hours of 7 May 1941 Widdows and Sergeant Ryall were vectored towards a bandit over the Channel. As Widdows continued to alter their position in search of the enemy, Ryall spotted a Junkers Ju 88 silhouetted against a thin layer of cloud and prompted Widdows to dive. Still, the Ju 88 proved elusive, until visual contact was made a second time. Widdows fired from approximately 100 yards at the 88's starboard engine, which burst into flames. In retaliation, the Ju 88's rear gunner sprayed the attacking Beaufighter and scored hits on the cockpit instrument panel, blowing away the intercom switch and striking Widdows in the left leg. The Junkers banked away to the left, while the front gunner continued to fire at Widdows as he passed underneath it. Breaking off from the engagement, Widdows landed at West Malling without the use of his flaps and brakes. On landing he found that his observer, 25-year-old Browne Ryall, was missing. Sadly, Ryall was never found. ∎

....

Combat Report 7.5.41

I was ordered on patrol under Kenley and handed over to Moleskin, when I was put on to one raid but lost it on reaching the coast. I was then vectored around and eventually told another bandit was approaching. I vectored 150 for some time and was brought round on to bandit who was reported flying at 16,000 ft. on a course of 45 degrees. I flashed but no contact and then was told by Moleskin I had overshot, so I turned round to port and in doing so my observer saw bandit flying at about 3/4000 ft. below us. I did a diving turn and straightened up on observer's instructions on approx. course of bandit, he incidentally having lost visual contact on the turn. I was again told by Moleskin that I was behind E/A. A.I. operator eventually picked up blip and directed me to starboard. After further directions I obtained visual contact and closed to about 100 yards when I opened fire and the starboard engine caught fire and there was considerable return fire. The E/A banked to left and appeared to be gradually losing height but I made straight for home having been hit in my left leg. On landing I found my A.I. operator missing.

....

Warrant Officer
David Denchfield

SGT/PILOT
DAVID DENCHFIELD
601 SQN

H.D Denchfield

David Pritchard

I T WOULD BE ABOUT DECEMBER 1938 THAT I RECEIVED all the bumph regarding the RAFVR and began explaining to Mum and Dad it was safer than the RAF, for we flew little aircraft, and yes if war came the RAF would mobilise me, but then I would be called up in any case from civvy street and that might be into the Army! It was a long haul, which went on until just after the New Year before Dad saw sense and signed the forms for me, and I sent them off in about early February 1939. In April I received my answer from the RAF telling me to report to the Town Centre of the No: E&RFTS, RAFVR in Bute Street, Luton on 18th May

"There was a sudden staccato vibration and sparks seemed to erupt out of my port wingtip."

1939, for medical and suitability checks. At about 5.30 pm a lad named Browne and myself were the last ones to be ruled fit and proper to join the RAFVR and were duly attested and sworn in to serve King and Country."

In the winter months of 1940–1, David Denchfield served with No. 610 Squadron, flying Spitfires. Reflecting upon those cold early mornings at readiness, Denchfield recalls:

Most mornings I was awakened at about 6 am, while it was still pitch black, hearing, half awake, the first uncertain coughing of a Merlin followed by the sudden rasping roar as she caught, reducing to a subdued rumble as the erk throttled back to let her warm, and sat waiting for the temperatures to stabilise before starting his checks. This sole engine would be followed by others in quick succession until a steady throb of maybe 12 to 14 Merlins intruded into that delightful hiatus twixt waking and sleeping. The Taffy would bring the tea, and say 'readiness in 5 minutes'. There followed 5 delicious minutes sitting drinking tea exchanging the odd monosyllabic comment with Billy Raine or Sam Hamer if they were also on readiness, and then the shocking plunge out into the freezing atmosphere beyond the blankets. A quick wash and shave, dress in the 'working blue'; throw on the Irving leather jacket and then the crunching walk across the iron-hard airfield at B dispersal. Then into the harsh glare of the bare electric light bulbs of the Nissen hit, grunt a sort of 'wot ho' to whoever happened to be there, and picking up one's brolly amble across the 200 yards of frosted grass and mud to aircraft DW-P.

On 5 February 1941 No. 610 Squadron was ordered to fly as fighter escort to twelve Blenheims that were detailed to bomb the airfield at Saint-Omer. On this occasion Denchfield flew as 'weaver', which positioned him to the rear of the Squadron. Once over the French coast, Denchfield reported some contrails over to the left and slightly behind the Squadron's position. The contrails quickly extinguished, which meant that whatever was causing them was now either above or below the contrail level. Suddenly, Denchfield saw a flash somewhere above and behind him. Moments later Denchfield became separated from the rest of his Squadron and was soon under attack.

There was a sudden staccato vibration and sparks seemed to erupt out of my port wingtip. My 'bloody hell' and steep left hand turn initiation only just beat a violent clang from up front, at which the rudder pedals suddenly lost all feel and became seemingly disconnected from the rudder. As the nose fell away, the cockpit filled with a white mist accompanied by a foul smell of glycol and 100-octane fuel. I let the nose go down, hoping whatever it was couldn't follow.

After a rapid descent, Denchfield's Spitfire caught fire, leaving him with no other option but to bale out.

Upon landing, Denchfield buried his chute in 18-inch-deep snow and attempted to hide behind some nearby bushes before two German uniforms approached him. 'As I stood up the one holding the gun said: "For you the war is over." And I thought they only said that in things like the Hotspur and Magnet. We live and learn.' ∎

Flight Lieutenant
Jimmy Corbin, DFC

P/O JIMMY CORBIN

66 SQDN

Jimmy Corbin

DAVIP RICHARD

IN APRIL 1939 WILLIAM JAMES CORBIN JOINED THE RAFVR and began flying in Rochester. He was called up on 1 September, and joined No. 74 Squadron at Kirton-in Lindsey on 26 August 1940. Three days later he moved to Coltishall to join No. 66 Squadron. Thereafter Corbin was posted to No. 610 stationed at Acklington.

After a lively night out in Newcastle, where many drinks had been consumed by the boys of No. 610 Squadron, the quietness of the dispersal hut was an appreciated gesture. Sergeant Jimmy Corbin was sitting in a comfortable armchair, wrestling with the early morning tension of readiness, when the telephone snapped him out of his thoughts. The Flight Commander shouted instructions for Blue Section to push off.

Corbin was soon flying as Blue 3 in vic formation, climbing to a height of 20,000 feet. The Spitfires soared with eloquent beauty, intent on protecting the Tyneside shipyards from droning German bombers. Passing

The three Spitfires swooped down like birds of prey and circled the seaplane at 1,000 feet, forcing it to keep still.

through patches of grey cloud, Corbin began to feel taut. Flying into the unknown was always daunting, and fear was ever present. On reaching its destination, Blue Section patrolled the misty sky in a circle, searching for lurking bandits. Constantly twisting and turning their heads, the pilots thoroughly checked the proximity for enemy aircraft. Clusters of cumulus cloud limited visibility. The CO dropped below the cloud line, leading the Spitfires out towards the North Sea. As the sky cleared, the CO finally caught sight of a bandit down below and notified Blue 2 and 3. Corbin turned his aircraft slightly and looked down at the cold sea. Just off the Northumbrian coast, he spotted the Heinkel 115 seaplane, taxiing along a small land mass. The three Spitfires swooped down like birds of prey and circled the seaplane at 1,000 feet, forcing it to keep still. Blue section held the Heinkel prisoner until a naval warship arrived and captured the German crew.

Corbin's uneasiness was replaced with accomplishment. They had stopped a Heinkel without firing a single round.

By June 1941 Corbin was flying Spitfire Mk IIs, having rejoined No. 66 Squadron. On the 25th, flying with Squadron Leader Athol Forbes as Red 2, Corbin searched for an apparently lost Heinkel He 111 over the Channel. Corbin's combat report detailed the interception.

....

Combat Report 25.6.41

```
RED.2. At 04.45 hours I took off with Red
1 for an interception patrol. We vectored
110 at Angels 3 and then turned South of
Plymouth Balloon Barrage when we were
vectored 140° at gate. The angels of the
bandit were given at 1 1/2 We reduced height
and when at Pt.6 I sighted an aircraft
ahead about 2 miles S.E. of Pt.5. I
notified Red 1 who instructed me to lead.
I gradually overtook and delivered a
forward quarter attack developing into
a quarter for about 3 seconds breaking
to port. Red.1 then attacked from port.
I then attacked from port and once more
from starboard when due to the bad light
and visibility I lost the bandit. The
bandit was flying at about 50 feet and
travelling 240-260 m.p.h and could only
be seen from the south against the gradual
rising sun. Our port attacks were judged
from the other fire. There was high 10/10
cloud with 7/10 low cloud with a top of
about 700 feet. Towards the end of the
combat we ran into low sea mist and looking
towards the south visibility was about 500
yards and towards the rising sun about
1 1/2 miles. Fairly inaccurate fire was
experienced from the rear gunner.
```

....

During his time with No. 66 Squadron, Corbin became one of the 'Ten Fighter Boys', after recording his personal experiences in a book published while the bombs were still falling and the aerial conflict was still raging overhead. ∎

Flight Lieutenant
Trevor Gray

PILOT OFFICER
TREVOR GRAY 64 SQN.

DAVID PRITCHARD.

IN SEPTEMBER 1940 PILOT OFFICER TREVOR GRAY joined No. 64 Squadron at Leconfield in Yorkshire to fly Spitfires. The Squadron had been sent north to catch its breath after an exhausting fight on the front line, but the move was not without incident. During an interception patrol, the Squadron sniffed out a lone Bf 110 performing a reconnaissance mission. Gray attacked the intruder first, damaging its port under-carriage, before others from the Squadron staked their claims. Irrespective of its wounds, the 110 managed to limp home, streaming glycol.

Although this particular event remains clear in Gray's mind, the 'most remembered episode', as Trevor recalls, came some time after this engagement:

It is perhaps not surprising that after seventy years the experiences of the Battle of Britain period are no longer remembered as discrete incidents, but have melded together into an amorphous memory of the period as a whole. However, there is one memory that remains complete and

"It only took a moment or two of rational thought, of course, to realise the awful truth: that the two pilots had collided..."

sharp and I believe will until the last memory cell has gone. It occurred in the early spring of 1941, when No. 64 Squadron, to which I was at the time attached, was stationed at Coltishall. Conditions were generally quiet at the time but there was a fair amount of convoy traffic in the Channel, which we patrolled frequently while hoping that the controller would find a 'bogie'. This did occur occasionally. One day we received the order to scramble the readiness section, which I happened to be leading, the two other members of the section being new pilots who had just joined the Squadron from Operational Training Unit and so were totally without any operational experience although fully trained to Squadron standards.

We duly took off and the Controller began the attempt to vector us towards where he believed the 'bogie' to be while we searched the skies. A very bright sun made searching quite tricky even for an experienced pilot. At the time we were flying as a loose vic, but my assessment was that some advantage in search capability might be obtained from a change to echelon starboard. I therefore gave the routine order 'echelon starboard, go'. This would prompt the Port wingman

to carry out a manœuvre that had been practised many times and should have been automatic. During the transition the leader can no longer see the transition as it happens, so when I judged the move should be complete I looked round to confirm that all was well. To my complete astonishment, where I expected to see three aircraft in echelon starboard the only aircraft visible was my own. It is beyond my ability to describe my emotions at that moment. To be leading a section of three aircraft and suddenly find that two have disappeared without trace is, to say the least, unnerving. It only took a moment or two of rational thought, of course, to realise the awful truth: that the two pilots had collided destructively. In spite of an extensive search, nothing was found, the incident being classed as an accident due to inexperience. I was unhappy about the outcome and decided to look at some of the factors that could have had an effect, in case I had been in any way deficient. Although the pilots were new, they were fully trained, and the type of sortie was the usual procedure when new pilots arrived. The formation change was routine and well practised during flying training, while the weather was quite outside our control. It must be conceded that, although they were 'fully trained', it is unlikely that the new pilots had reached a point at which control of the aircraft had become automatic and instinctive, and so full concentration would not have been available for the manœuvre being carried out. Given the conditions prevailing, a change in the effect of the sun at a critical moment, coupled with inexperience, could well have prompted a false move, with the tragic results that followed. I am therefore satisfied that my own performance cannot be criticised and am content that the official finding of 'accident due to inexperience' can be regarded as the final outcome. ■

Squadron Leader
Neville Duke,
DSO, DFC**, OBE, AFC, Military Cross (Czech)

Neville Duke joined No. 92 Squadron after the Battle of Britain in 1941. He was 19 years of age when he arrived at Biggin Hill and quickly became accustomed to the Squadron's practices. He spent many joyous evenings with the boys of 92, drinking at the White Hart and dancing with the local girls. It was a crack squadron and Duke was more than happy to be flying Spitfires over Kent with capable and experienced fighter pilots such as 'Titch' Havercroft and Geoffrey Wellum. Duke's operational duties began gradually, but he was soon in the deep end. On Saturday, 26 April, Duke was involved in an early afternoon sweep over the Channel at 32,000 feet. The Squadron was vectored towards enemy aircraft, and Duke soon spotted a bunch of Messerschmitt 109s fighting with a flight of Hurricanes. Duke caught a fighter in his gunsight as it dived for the sea and fired a steady burst. The 109's exhaust licked with flame, but another Spitfire cut between Duke and the 109, so he was forced to break away without seeing any further

Because of the immense airspeed he had clocked up in pursuit of the 109s, Duke blacked out and narrowly avoided stalling his engine.

results of his attack. As first combat experiences go, it was not a bad one. Duke had hit a 109 and, more importantly, he had survived his first encounter with the enemy.

On 25 June 1941 Pilot Officer Neville Duke took part in a midday 'Circus' sortie with the Squadron, accompanied by No. 609 and No. 74 Squadrons. The three fighter units were flying as top cover to an armada of Blenheims over Saint-Omer at around 30,000 feet. Inevitably they were greeted by Messerschmitt 109s and immediately put to work.

Flying as No. 2 to Allan Wright, Duke dived with his section leader after two 109s, but soon found that they could not catch them. Promptly pulling out of their dives, the 109s climbed back up into the sky, which caused Duke to break away. Because of the immense airspeed he had clocked up in pursuit of the 109s, Duke blacked out and narrowly avoided stalling his engine. In a matter of seconds he was back to his senses and climbing for height.

Duke witnessed Allan Wright diving with a 109 that was pouring glycol before he himself was attacked by a couple of fighters from astern. Fortunately seeing the 109s just in time, Duke turned his Spitfire and saw the flash of tracer whistle past his aircraft.

Arriving over Dunkirk, Duke passed two 109s and then turned to see a dogfight taking place near Dunkirk. The Spitfire pilot flew back into action. Duke's combat report describes what happened next.

....

```
Combat Report for 25 June
Time: 1245 hrs off Dunkirk

When at sea level flying west of Dunkirk,
I looked back and saw six Me109s having a
dog-fight with two Spitfires. I turned and
joined in and managed to get on the tail
of one 109F which was on the tail of a
Spitfire. I opened fire with cannons and
machine-guns and gave him two bursts and
closed to 50 yards, when I had to pull
away as I got into his slipstream.

I came back on top of him and saw the
pilot sitting quite quietly without looking
around or up and proceeded to go down in a
gentle dive from 2,000 feet, and hit the
ground just east of Dunkirk and blow up.

On my way back I saw two orange-coloured
parachutes going down, but no persons
attached. I also saw four ships of about
1,000 tons escorted by four E-boats.
```
....

After watching the 109 crash a few miles inland, Duke sped for home at sea level. It had been a stressful encounter for both the pilot and his aircraft. When Duke touched down on the aerodrome, his engine stopped for lack of petrol. ■

Squadron Leader
William John Johnson, DFC*

Wg Cdr W. Johnson DFC
85 and 145 Sqns

DavidPritchard

A T 19 YEARS OF AGE, 'JOHNNY' JOHNSON JOINED the RAFVR in Northampton as a Sergeant Pilot and was called up in 1939, to begin his flying training. After flying in primary training aircraft, Johnson converted to Hawker Hurricanes and, after just eleven hours flying them, he was posted to an operational squadron towards the end of the Battle of Britain.

In mid-October 1940 Johnson joined No. 145 Squadron stationed at Tangmere, and three months later he had his first flight in a Supermarine Spitfire.

At around 1230 hours on 26 June 1941, Johnson was flying with No. 145 Squadron's A Flight over the French coast, when he noticed a Messerschmitt 109F diving towards his unsuspecting section from approximately 21,000 feet. Warning the other pilots over the R/T, Johnson managed to line the 109 up in his sights as it dived across his line of fire. Giving the machine a short burst, Johnson observed accurate and deadly hits as his ammunition caused substantial damage to the enemy aircraft, surely putting it out of action.

On 22 October 1941 Squadron Leader P. S. Turner noted in Johnson's log book: 'Sgt W. J. Johnson is at present the oldest member of the squadron and during the time I have commanded it I have found him to be an above-the-average pilot and a good reliable leader.'

When this entry was made Johnson was only 22 years of age.

In October 2010, William Johnson's son, Alan Johnson, MBE, recalled the following about his father:

Squadron Leader W. J. Johnson, DFC and Bar (1919–96), known in his early RAF life as Bill but known to me as Dad and to his wife and friends as Johnny, was a caring father and a loving husband, who loved aircraft, whose career was in the RAF and later the Air Ministry. I have clear memories of him being in charge of No. 74 Squadron at Horsham St Faith (Norwich) and also at this time the Leader of an

…Johnson managed to line the 109 up in his sights as it dived across his line of fire.

RAF aerobatic team flying Meteor 8s. My Father declined to talk about his wartime experiences with me. I remember one day when I pressed him he said, 'Do you want me to tell you about the time my friend baled out and was shot by German

fighters or the time I dived and shot up a parade of German soldiers?' We never mentioned it again. Since he died I have found out much more about what he did during the Second World War while flying Hurricanes and then Spitfires.

Reading his log book of his time in Malta (7 May 1942–17 Aug. 1942) made me very proud of him. He journeyed from England to Gibraltar, where they picked up boxed Spitfires, which were assembled on the way to Malta and then flown off HMS Eagle as soon as they were within flying range, without any previous testing. Their ammunition bays were full of cigarettes and chocolates for those in Malta.

After a four-hour flight, Johnson recorded the following in his log book: 'I should have taken some Bovril before taking off!!! Attacked by 109s on landing in circuit!!!' ■

The following combat report, written by William John Johnson towards the end of June 1941, is a rare find.

Combat Report 26.6.41

```
I was yellow two flying in circles on June
26th and was flying over the French coast
near Dunkerque with the wing and climbing
to join four other Spitfires when I
noticed an a/c diving on them from above
and slightly behind. I recognised the a/c
as a 109f and called to the four Spitfires
who seemed not to have noticed the 109.
The enemy did not fire on the formation
but dived fast turning slightly, diving
down straight in front of me at a distance
of about 100 yds. I gave a burst of about
2 seconds and saw huge pieces fly off the
tail and the cockpit cover came off and
the a/c continued its dive into the cloud.
The pilot did not bale out.
```

Squadron Leader
Percy Beake, DFC

PILOT OFFICER
PERCIVAL BEAKE
64 SQN.

PERCY BEAKE WAS BORN IN MONTREAL, CANADA OF Bristolian parents on 17 March 1917. In April 1939 he joined the RAFVR and went on to complete almost fifty hours flying Tiger Moths. In September 1940 Beake joined No. 64 Squadron at Leconfield and served with the Squadron during the Battle of Britain, mostly flying convoy protection patrols. Reflecting upon his time as a Spitfire pilot, Percy recalls an alarming flight that occurred on 2 February 1941:

We were returning from an operational patrol and a sweep of the French coast when, having crossed the English coastline, our Flight Commander called us in to tight formation. We were heading for our temporary base at Rochford and seemed to be making very slow progress — maybe a strong headwind was responsible. We had been airborne for longer than usual and I was getting concerned about my fuel usage especially since I was flying a brand new Spitfire Mk II which had been allocated to me on the previous day. The Spitfire's fuel gauge is not a continuously registering one — a button had to be pressed to activate it. To take your eyes off an aircraft on which you are closely formatting is not to be recommended! However my concern was such that I pulled away from my leader to allow me safely to do this and was horrified to see that my tank was almost empty. I radioed my Flight Commander and said I was breaking away because of fuel shortage and immediately started looking for an aerodrome on which I could land. I couldn't see one so I turned my attention to finding a large, level field on which I could try

"This made the port wing dig into the ground; it was torn off and caused the plane to roll over so that I was now skidding along on my head..."

a wheels down landing. However, all such fields had obstructions placed across them to prevent enemy gliders from landing. My engine cut and I had to make a quick decision.

My concern for my new Spitfire transcended that of my own safety. I spotted a reasonably sized field and decided to try a wheels down landing even though it was surrounded by trees. On my gliding approach I could see that these trees were much taller than I had expected. So as I crossed them I put my aircraft into a sideslip to get down quickly but was just a little late in levelling out with the result that my port

wheel hit the ground first and buckled under the aircraft. This made the port wing dig into the ground; it was torn off and caused the plane to roll over so that I was now skidding along on my head and thought that I would surely collide with something that would end my life. However, the plane eventually stopped and I was surprised to be still alive. I was of course virtually helpless — just able to release my safety straps and free myself from my seat. The cockpit of a Spitfire is quite small and there was little room to move. My great fear was that a fire might break out and I would be completely trapped. However, as time went by and there was no sound or smell of a fire (no doubt because I had run out of petrol) I began to relax. I had landed in Shepherdswell in Kent and an army camp was not far away so it was not long before I heard voices and the sound of running feet. When the runners were at the aircraft I shouted out to tell them that I was still alive and not badly injured. I persuaded someone to put their hand into the cockpit and feel around for the lever on the flap cover which we climbed into and got out of the airplane. Seeing the position, some soldiers went around to the tip of the inverted starboard wing and weighed down on it to roll the fuselage over to give more room for me to be pulled out by my extended arm. Apart from my skinned forehead, I felt reasonably well but I was concussed and was sent to the RAF Officer's Hospital in Torquay. I returned to the Squadron on 27 March — an absence of over seven weeks. ■

Group Captain
Byron Duckenfield, AFC

FLYING OFFICER
BYRON DUCKENFIELD
74 AND 501 SQNS

ON 28 DECEMBER 1942 SQUADRON LEADER Byron Duckenfield sat attentively in the snug cockpit of his Hurricane IIC as first light began to crack open the sky at Chittagong in the early hours of a humid morning.

By this time the experienced fighter pilot from Sheffield was well accustomed to dawn readiness and operational sorties, having previously served with Nos 32 and 501 Squadrons during the Battle of Britain. He had already flown many strenuous patrols against the Luftwaffe over the Channel and southern parts of Britain, so Duckenfield was fully aware of the dangers inflicted upon those who sported white wings on their blue RAF uniforms. The difference for Duckenfield now was not only a new enemy but also a new battleground.

During the Battle of Britain British pilots were fighting over their homeland, so, if they ran into trouble, they were generally comforted by the knowledge that they were descending over friendly ground. Fighting overseas, however, was an utterly different affair.

With a mission to fly to central Burma to attack the Japanese airbase at Magwe, 300 miles away on the banks of the River Irrawaddy, Duckenfield took off, leading eleven other Hurricanes in his wake. While climbing for height in his aircraft, armed with years of operational experience, Duckenfield was not prepared for what was about to happen. Duckenfield remarked:

Arriving at Yenangyaung, we turned downstream at minimum height for Magwe, 30 miles to the south, and jettisoned drop tanks. Just before sighting the enemy base, the squadron climbed to 1,200 feet and positioned to attack from up-sun. On the ramp at the base, in front of the hangers, were 10 or 12 Nakajima Ki-43 'Oscars' in rough line-up (not dispersed), perhaps readying for take-off. These aircraft, and the hangers behind them, were attacked in a single pass, before we withdrew westward at low level and maximum speed.

A few minutes later, perhaps already 20 miles away from Magwe, I was following the line of a chaung [small creek], height about 250 feet, speed about 280 mph, when the aircraft gave a violent shudder, accompanied by a very loud, unusual noise. The cause was instantly apparent: the airscrew had disappeared completely, leaving only a spinning hub. Immediate reaction was to throttle back fully and switch off to stop the violently over-speeding engine. Further action was obvious: I was committed to staying with the aircraft because, even with a high initial speed, not enough height to eject could be gained without the help of an airscrew. So, I jettisoned the canopy and acknowledged gratefully the fact that I was following the creek; the banks on either side were hillocky ground, hostile to a forced-landing aircraft. Flying the course of the creek, I soon found the aircraft to be near the stall (luckily, a lower-than-normal figure without an airscrew), extended the flaps and touched down wheels-up with minimum impact (I have done worse landings on a smooth runway!)

My luck was holding, if one can talk of luck in such a situation. December is the height of the dry season in that area and the creek had little water, it was shallow and narrow at the point where I came down; shallow enough to support the fuselage and narrow enough to support wingtips. So, I released the harness, pushed the IFF 'Destruct' switch, climbed out and walked the wing ashore, dry-shod. The question may occur: 'Why did not others in the Squadron see their leader go down?' The answer is simple: the usual tactic on withdrawal from an enemy target was to fly singly at high speed and low level on parallel courses until a safe distance from target was attained. Then, the formation would climb to reassemble.

Having left the aircraft, I now faced a formidable escape problem: I was 300 miles from friendly territory: my desired route would be westward, but 80 per cent of that 300 miles was covered by steep north–south ridges impenetrably clothed in virgin jungle. These were natural impediments; there was also the enemy to consider. Before we had taken off that morning, I had been worrying over administrative issues, such as providing a roof for the airmen's cookhouse to prevent kite hawks from stealing the food. Now, I had only myself to worry about. Having thought over my predicament, I decided the best I could do — having heard reports of mean-hearted plainspeople — was to get as far into the hills as possible and then find a (hopefully sympathetic) village. I suppose I may have covered about 15 miles by nightfall, when I came upon this small hill village and walked into the village square. Nobody seemed surprised to see me (I suspect I had been followed for some time); I was given a quiet welcome, seated at a table in the open and given food. Then, exhaustion took over, I fell asleep in the chair and woke later to find myself tied up in it.

Next day, I was handed over to a Japanese sergeant and escort who took me back to Magwe and, soon after that, two and a half years' captivity in Rangoon Jail. ∎

Flight Lieutenant
John 'Percy' Greenwood

JOHN GREENWOOD SERVED WITH NO. 253 SQUADRON in France and throughout the Battle of Britain. The following extract, written by Greenwood himself, details an honest opinion of his impressions of the Squadron and his superiors.

As the last remaining pilot left alive from the formation of 253 Squadron to 31 October 1940 (the end of the Battle of Britain), I think a short history of all our Commanding Officers and the cavalier way in which we were treated by our superiors should be recorded before we are all dead. These opinions are my own; but they are as honest and true as I can remember.

253 Squadron was formed in November 1939 at Manston, and our first CO (Commanding Officer) was S/Leader Elliot, who had been in the RAF for some years and was one of the first pilots to land on an aircraft carrier. He re-equipped with brand new aircraft having rotol props, two new flight commanders and a new CO, who was S/Leader David Atcherly, the younger of two brothers notorious in the pre-war RAF for their crazy stunts. He was an imposing character, in looks similar to Julius Caesar, with a fine roman nose. This was not the type of CO that was needed at the moment. We were very low in morale; those of us who had returned from France were lucky to have survived and had discovered that the Me l09 was a much superior fighter than a Hurricane. The pilot replacements we received were from OTU's with only a few hours on Hurricanes; us old hands had to train them, while at the same time the battle over Dunkirk was evolving. David Atcherly was on the phone to all his mates in Group Air Ministry so that he could lead the Squadron over Dunkirk, while we were quaking in our shoes that we would have to lead some highly untrained boys into the inferno. Fortunately for us, the leaders in Fighter

"We were very low in morale; those of us who had returned from France were lucky to have survived and had discovered the Me 109 was a much superior fighter than the Hurricane."

was quite conservative, not 'hail fellow and well met'. We did not see a lot of him in our spare time. On 15 May, while stationed at Kenley, five days after the invasion of France, 'B' Flight were ordered out to Lille Marqe in France with F/Lt Anderson as our commander. Six aircraft flew there. S/Leader Elliot, his Adjutant and the Intelligence Officer all stayed at Kenley. After three days in France we were surrounded and ordered home to Kenley on 19 May. Three aircraft flew back in the late afternoon. F/Lt Anderson and F/Sgt McKenzie had been shot down and killed and P/O Jenkins's aircraft was unserviceable by enemy fire and chopped up by axe.

The next two days we operated from Kenley over the coast of France. On the 21st, while on patrol over Arras and Cambrai, S/Leader Elliot disappeared; we saw no enemy fighters, only heavy flak. He was posted as missing. (He force-landed 'undamaged' in France and spent the rest of the war as a POW.)

On 24 May, 253 Squadron moved from Kenley to Kirton-in-Lindsey to re-form. In the previous week we had lost our CO (missing), both flight commanders (one killed, one wounded) and six other pilots. (It should be noted that the Hurricanes that 253 flew in France were the original aircraft that formed 253 Squadron; canvas wings and airframe, two-blade fixed pitch propeller, no armour plating and no mirrors.) Within the next few days we started to be

Command knew what was going on, and within a few days S/Ldr Atcherly was posted to Wick in the north of Scotland. We were never so happy to see anyone leave us as him. We did hear (but I cannot vouch for the truth) that while in Wick he took off in a Magister and against all the signals landed on the deck of an Aircraft Carrier and went down the Aircraft Carrier Lift, which was down at the time. Our next CO, who arrived in early June, was the complete opposite to David Atcherly; he was S/Leader Tom Gleave. In his early 30s, he had been in a desk job, but had been pulling all the strings he could to get into a squadron. He was a gentleman and a lovely personality. Although he would have loved to 'hit the Hun over Dunkirk', he realised the totally traumatised situation of 253 Squadron, with himself and both flight commanders having never seen any enemy action and half the squadron with only a few hours on Hurricanes; he relied on the few of us still left from the French debacle to help train and inform the remainder of the pilots in respect to the Luftwaffe. Kirton-in-Lindsey was in the centre of several Bomber Stations and we liaised with them for practice attacks. We had become once more a cohesive squadron until suddenly in mid-July we were presented with a new CO — S/Leader Eric King. S/Ldr Gleave stayed as supernumerary. Nobody knew quite what was to happen now. Shortly after, 253 Squadron moved to Turnhouse on 23 July, and on 5 August S/Leader King was posted away to 249 Squadron.

In the short time he was with us, he acted very strangely, keeping to himself and seemed to be going through some sort of a break-down. (Within the month he was killed as CO of 151 Squadron, from an unknown cause). We breathed a sigh of relief when S/Leader King left us, but within three days a new CO arrived to take over from S/Leader Gleave, who remained as a supernumerary CO. The new CO was S/Leader Starr — he came from 245 Squadron; but, like all our other COs, he had no battle experience. This unsettled the squadron again, as we all liked Tom Gleave. However, he settled in quite well and was eager to learn from us. On 23 August, 253 Squadron moved again to Prestwick and then on 29 August we again moved; this time at last to join in the Battle of Britain at Kenley. Next day, 30 August, between 10.50 a.m. and 11.20 a.m. nineteen aircraft of 253 went forth into battle. From that first sortie three aircraft were shot down, two pilots killed, one in hospital; several aircraft were damaged, including S/Leader Starr's. Next morning of 31 August S/Leader Starr was killed and replaced by S/Leader Gleave, who was shot down and badly burnt on the afternoon of 31 August. He was replaced on 1 September by F/Lt Cambridge, who had been 'B' Flight Commander. He carried on until 5 September, when he was shot down and killed. He was replaced by S/Leader Edge, who came from 605 Squadron and was our first CO who had experienced enemy action. He was quite a feisty little man and took no nonsense, but was easily the best leader that 253 had had since its formation. Unfortunately he was shot down in the Channel on 26 September and hospitalised. The senior F/Lt became acting CO. He was F/Lt Duke-Woolly with no fighter experience. He had come from 25 Squadron on Blenheims: he was a poor leader, but remained until after 31 October, when the Battle of Britain officially ended.

Almost seventy years after this momentous year, living on the opposite side of the world, I am still angry at the way the administrators of our country treated 253 Squadron. Of the nine COs allotted to the Squadron, only one was experienced and led us well into battle. During the period from 15 May to 30 October, 253 Squadron lost almost two complete flying squadrons in killed and wounded, but inflicted more on the Luftwaffe. In all that time not one DFC was awarded to any pilot in the squadron. I do not know of any other Squadron being treated so badly. We were sent to France at one hour's notice and told to take all our belongings with us. A few days later my belongings were at the bottom of Boulogne Harbour, where they remain to this day. We were left with what we stood up in. Our grateful country gave all who had lost their kit £25 to replace it (a greatcoat cost

more than that alone). In France, except for the Flight Commander, who had an all-metal plane with constant speed prop, the other five pilots had old Hurricanes with canvas fuselage and wings, fix pitch wooden prop, NO armour plating, NO mirrors. My plane number was L1712, which will show its age for those interested. The few of us who returned from France had learned much, the most important being that the Me 109 was a much better war plane than the Hurricane in all departments except manœuvrability. We

"We learned not to think we were invincible and not to make head-on attacks against Me 109s or Me 110s"

learned not to think we were invincible and not to make head-on attacks against Me 109s or Me 110s. If they are above you and attack while you are on the climb, run for your life. That is why I am still alive, as these are the rules I obeyed. Plus a little luck! As you see, I am one of the few people who do not think Dowding was a genius; he was as much to blame as anyone, that we had inferior planes and armament to the Germans. Also, he should have stopped wasting our trained pilots and aircraft in France. They were not withdrawn until his superior Air Chief Marshal Newell ordered him to. That fact is not known by most people. ■

Epilogue

ON **10 SEPTEMBER 2010** WING COMMANDER JOHN FREEBORN'S LIFE was celebrated by his family and friends at the Southport Crematorium. It was a sombre morning with heavy rain and thunderous skies that seemed to bemoan his passing. As I watched John's coffin, draped in a Union Jack, arrive at the Crematorium, I felt immensely proud to have been a friend of such a brilliant and charismatic man as John. The service itself was full of tributes to John's RAF career, particularly his exploits during 1940. As I reflected on John's experiences, I began to appreciate how truly fortunate I was to have been able to listen to them at first hand over the years.

When I was at North Weald with John in 2009, visiting the grave of Pilot Officer Montague Hulton-Harrop (the first RAF fighter pilot casualty of the Second World War), John told the BBC: 'I've had a good life, and he should have had a good life, too.'

The 'Few' were 2,353 young men from Great Britain and 574 from overseas who are recognised for having taken part in the Battle of Britain (10 July– 31 October 1940). During this period of conflict, 544 airmen lost their lives, but many more were burned, maimed and scarred fighting for Britain's preservation. While it is of high importance to remember the stories of those who survived, John's statement prompts us also to remember those who gave the ultimate sacrifice for their country. The summer and autumn of 1940 is a timeframe enriched with bravery, selflessness and sacrifice.

One such act of selflessness was exemplified by Flight Lieutenant James Nicolson of No. 249 Squadron on the afternoon of 16 August near Southampton. While climbing to 17,500 feet with the sun behind his section of three Hurricanes, Nicolson, flying as Red 1, heard Yellow Leader call 'Tally Ho!' over the R/T. Moments after the call, Nicolson's section was bounced, and his cockpit was struck by four successive cannon shells. The first shell ripped through the cockpit hood, showering Nicolson with splinters of Perspex, one of which pierced his left eyelid, causing blood to stream down his face, obscuring his vision. Another shell shattered his left heel, numbing his foot and shredding his uniform. But, worst of all, one shell punctured his reserve petrol tank, which was situated in front of the pilot. Horrifying flames began to lick into the cockpit, so Nicolson pulled his feet up onto his seat and rammed the stick forward to put the Hurricane's nose down and into a steep dive to starboard to evade his attacker. With his Hurricane ablaze and travelling at around 400 mph, Nicolson prepared to evacuate his aircraft, until he saw a Bf 110 whizz past him. Astonishingly, Nicolson stayed in the hot furnace of a cockpit and opened fire at the 110 at a range of about 200 yards, thumbing the gun until he could no longer bear the intense heat. With some difficulty Nicolson abandoned his Hurricane, and, after falling about 5,000 feet, he pulled his ripcord. Nicolson's problems were not yet over. Just before he reached the ground, he was shot in the buttocks by a member of the Home Guard, who mistook him for a German pilot. Wounded and badly burned, James Nicolson was taken to hospital, where he would remain for some time. On 15 November 1940 he learned that he had been awarded the Victoria Cross for his gallantry in the air. It is reported that Nicolson remarked: 'Now I will have to go and earn it.'

Two days after Nicolson's escapade, another pilot displayed the same fighting spirit while leading No. 111 Squadron into an onslaught of Dorniers that were bombing Kenley at low level. Flight Lieutenant Stanley Connors, with twelve confirmed victories already to his credit, flew his Hurricane after the bombers, despite the hot zone of anti-aircraft fire exploding around them. His Hurricane was hit and caught fire, but Connors continued to blast away at a Dornier with fierce tenacity. His burning Hurricane crash-landed in an orchard north of Kenley airfield, and Connors was thrown from the cockpit. His body was later found by a member of the Home Guard, who had witnessed his last action.

There are hundreds of stories that ought to be remembered like Nicolson's and Connors's. During that violent conflict of 1940, many pilots were horrendously wounded, hideously burned and killed in both combat and flying accidents. Some were lost to the Channel, some crashed with their machines and others fell from the sky with unopened parachutes.

These iconic fighter pilots were mostly just regular young men who willingly accepted the call to arms. It is my hope that we may often remember those who lost their futures so that we can freely find our own.

Let us therefore brace ourselves to our duties, and so bear ourselves that, if the British Empire and its Commonwealth last for a thousand years, men will still say: 'This was their finest hour.'

(Winston Churchill, 18 June 1940)

Friends Remembered

By Flight Lieutenant William L. B. Walker

Some memories may diminish as we age
Though we shall ne'er forget those distant years
When deeds and daring filled our earthly stage
And all who flew were willing volunteers.

They never thought to count the cost
As youthful lives were severed in their prime
And well remembered friends were lost
Who had so many mountains still to climb.

We, who by good fortune did survive,
Remember having known them with pride
For in our hearts they still remain alive.
We glory in the cause for which they died.

Acknowledgements

With sincere appreciation, I would like to thank all of the pilots included in this book, for their inspiring stories and for kindly helping me gather the material needed for this project. My thanks extend to my father, Bob Yeoman, for his initiative in producing a brilliant collection of portraits, and to David Pritchard, who has superbly painted some of 'The Few' when they were young men in the Royal Air Force. I would like to thank Chris Barker, Alan Johnson and Arthur Westerhoff for their contributions and Steve Darlow for his valued assistance in the production of this book. I would also like to thank Hilary Walford for her editorial finesse. Finally, I am undoubtedly grateful to The National Archives for its excellent collection and the accessibility of its combat reports.

Bibliography

Manuscripts
The National Archives, Combat Reports.

Published Works
Addison, Paul, and Crang, Jeremy A., *The Burning Blue* (Pimlico, 2000).

Bungay, Stephen, *The Most Dangerous Enemy* (Aurum Press Ltd, 2001).

Corbin, Jimmy, *Last of the Ten Fighter Boys* (Sutton Publishing, 2007).

Darlow, Steve, *Five of the Few* (Grub Street, 2006).

Doe, Bob, *Fighter Pilot* (CCB Aviation Books, 1999).

Franks, Norman, *Hurricane at War: 2* (Ian Allan Ltd, 1986).

Franks, Norman, *The War Diaries of Neville Duke* (Grub Street, 1995).

Kingcome, Brian, *A Willingness to Die* (The History Press, 2006).

Lane, Brian, *Spitfire!* (Amberley Publishing, 2009).

Levine, Joshua, *Forgotten Voices of the Blitz and the Battle of Britain* (Ebury Press, 2006).

Mason, Francis K., *Battle over Britain* (Aston Publications Ltd, 1990).

Neil, Tom, *Gun-Button to 'Fire'* (William Kimber, 1987).

Palmer, Derek, *Fighter Squadron* (The Self Publishing Association, 1990).

Richey, Paul, *Fighter Pilot* (Cassell & Co, 2001).

Robinson, Michael, *Best of the Few* (Michael Robinson, 2001).

Ross, David, *Stapme* (Grub Street, 2002).

Thomas, Hugh, *Spirit of the Blue* (Sutton Publishing, 2004).

Watkins, David, *Fear Nothing* (Newton Publishers, 1990).

Wellum, Geoffrey, *First Light* (Viking, 2002).

Willis, John, *Churchill's Few* (Michael Joseph, 1985).

Wynn, Kenneth G., *Men of the Battle of Britain* (CCB Aviation Books, 1999).

Yeoman, Christopher, and Freeborn, John, *Tiger Cub* (Pen & Sword, 2009).

Index

A

B

C

D

E

F

G